Prayer That Heals Our Emotions

by
EDDIE ENSLEY

Foreword by Richard Rohr O.F.M.

CONTEMPLATIVE BOOKS

PRAYER THAT HEALS OUR EMOTIONS

Published by Contemplative Books
Box 8065, Columbus, GA, 31908

ISBN 0-939419-00-9

I dedicate this book to four caring friends whose love has made this book possible.

Harold McRae, Clair and Jerome Ennis and Judy Esway.

And in memory of my cousin, Bill Phelps, whose goodness touched countless lives. He was always for me, my big brother.

"sed ju'beas eam a sanctis angelis su'scipe et ad patriam paradisi perdu'ci"

Contents

Appendices

Acknowledgements

This book was completed during a time of family tragedy; one close relative died suddenly and unexpectedly. Another was killed in an automobile accident that critically injured another relative. In the midst of the pain and grief I drew closer to my family, especially my parents. My father's manly tenderness and gentleness has healed and sustained me all my life.

My mother's strength, understanding and ferocious ability to love and care is a treasure I cherish. And the courage of my Aunt Margaret and my cousin Gay Phelps in the midst of loss is a deep inspiration.

Foreword

"Shimmering. Yes, like swimming in moonlight," that is how the Cherokee Indian, Dane, describes the real world, which is the spiritual world. It is a world that Western people have very little contact with in the modern age. It is lost to the consciousness and desire of most people, except in the fleeting promises of preachers, in the hope awakened by authentic moments of love, and the now and then experience of wondrous awe before grandeur and unfathomability. But even these are not trusted or treasured!

We are a people who have largely defined ourselves outwardly. Within we feel out of control, denied, afraid, guilty, and on foreign soil. We try to compensate by self-help books and courses, by quick aphorisms, and falling back on the cultural and familial (and untested!) emotional responses. The result is that we are producing the greatest amount of material success along with the greatest amount of neurosis and interpersonal and spiritual failure in the very same group of people. We are educated for careers but not for the living of a full human life. Feelings are not "educated" at all, in fact, most people do not seem to know that it is possible. We must begin.

And there is a close and clear connection between our feeling function and our capacity for rich and authentic experience of the Holy. As Abraham Heshcel, the Jewish scholar, urgently taught: "the hour calls for a renewal of the antecedents of faith. . .because it is useless to offer conclusions of faith to those who do not the prerequisites." These necessary "antecedents of faith" are "certain insights, attitudes, and emotions...acts that happen within the depth of the person, moments that necessitate groping for faith." It is this rich wellspring of human emotion, where all human motivation, passion, and change begin, that Eddie Ensley seeks to uncover in these prayer exercises.

The Myers-Briggs Personality Profile, which has become so well known in church and professional circles, asserts that almost 75% of the general population fits into the "Sensate" typology. This means that the other 25% of "Intuitive" types, who have normally written the books of theology, meanings, and explanations, are probably not speaking very well to the mass of the population! Most of the world approaches reality in a hands-on, now, image oriented way. They are "sensates," who know through experience, detail, memory, through the concrete and the specific. This book is not theoretical at all, but immediatly leads the devoted reader to a concrete and image oriented prayer experience. There is no liberal or conservative theology to argue about, no denominational differences to debate. Eddie just says, "Let's pray and let God's action and presence speak for itself!" In that sense it is a risky and demanding book, a wonderful book.

After sixteen years on the road preaching myself, and fourteen years as a pastor of a lay community, I am painfully aware of how difficult it is to form people in a wholistic relationship to the Gospel. Some want prayer meetings, some want Scripture study, some want service and ministry, some want education, and some want consolation. Others want to be prophetic to the system, while others believe that religion is an inner affair of healing and personal wholeness. The health of this book is that all aspects of our life and the Gospel call are presented for consideration and healing. How good to see a book that can talk about inner healing, contemplation, sexual lovemaking, and nuclear disarmament under the same cover! These are signs of a maturing and adult Christianity that is unfolding in our time, despite all of the annoying evidence to the contrary. "For where sin abounds, there grace abounds even more." says St. Paul. (Romans 5:21).

May grace abound through these words and prayers ~ "yes, like swimming in moonlight" ~ the shimmering real world!

Fr. Richard Rohr, O.F.M.
New Jerusalem community
Cincinnati, Ohio

SECTION I
TOOLS FOR TRANSFORMATION

CHAPTER ONE

Healing The Hurt Places

As I was being introduced, I clutched tightly to a quarter in my pocket. Rubbing its rough edges against my fingers seemed to reduce my tension just a little. I am always a little tense before I speak, most speakers are; I believe they call it pre-performance anxiety. This time it overwhelmed me.

One of the members of the diocesan renewal committee that had invited us to do the retreat, a young family practice physician named Kate, had greeted me with scarcely veiled skepticism and hostility at supper. "Don't you think meditation should remain in the monasteries? I've always been taught meditation is for the very advanced. And here you are telling us about teenagers, housewives, and mechanics entering into the same prayer experiences the spiritual masters wrote about."

Her words had stung, and I let them throw me off balance. I was about to give the first session of a weekend retreat designed to lead people into deep inner peace and healing; even though at that moment my heart was far from peaceful.

I looked down into the audience at Kate's sterile, antiseptic expression that scarcely masked her skepticism and anger. I stumbled through the first few sentences; then realized that I couldn't finish the talk. I moved on to the guided prayer experience. I began playing a slow version of Bach's "Jesu" in the stereo system, as soft background to the meditation. I paused in the stillness and realized one more time that it was not my words or style or knowledge of

2.

theology that would bring healing, but God's all-feeling compassion and love. We were just providing the spiritual and emotional space for people to open up to that love.

As I began to enter into the quiet myself, my anxiety receded. I felt a loving and warming energy pour over me as if I were in a shower of light. I sensed others entering that shower of light together with me. Tears softly coursed down people's faces. A calmness thick with warmth and love came over us knitting our hearts together. Rather than being a solitary experience, it was as though in the silence we left behind the shattering distractions that keep us apart and we were now breathing one breath and experiencing the reality that one Heart beats in all of us. I gently and slowly continued the meditations, leading the group in remembering past joys and imagining a scene from Scripture.

Toward the end of the prayer experience, I noticed Kate, the young doctor, sobbing. Her's were not the shallow, tight, frantic sobs that come from hopelessness; but the deep purifying sobs that come from finally letting loose deeply entrenched pain.

After we finished the session, Kate took me aside and told me her story, letting me know what had happened to her during the prayer experience.

Her mother died of cancer when Kate was eight. In his grief, her father became more and more dependent on Kate, his only child, for emotional nurture; asking for an adult love that no little girl is capable of giving. His drinking habit developed into alcoholism. He abused her first with violent words then with violent actions. She showed me a scar on her hand from a cigarette burn, and another above her eye from a belt buckle.

A crash into a bridge abutment killed her father when she was eleven. A loving aunt reared her and sent her through school.

The shock, the scars of what had happened to her bored its way into the center of her being. Deep inside her heart she blamed herself for her father's death. Her emotions shut down, her personality became rigid. If only she had loved him enough, she had always thought.

She then told me what happened during the prayer experience:
"I felt an injection of love warming my heart, warming my body.

3.

When you asked us to remember joyful times, I went back to the time before my mother got sick. I saw the three of us happy, laughing enjoying homemade ice cream on the back porch. We were happy then.

"In that memory, for the first time in my adult life, I felt my daddy's love. I know he cared for me, cherished me. He just couldn't handle mother's death. I felt grief and pain too, grief that he is gone, grief that he didn't recover. The hurt and the grief I felt as we prayed were immense, but the sense of love and caring were even greater."

Kate continued the journey that began during the retreat. She started seeing a Christian psychotherapist so the healing would continue. She initiated a daily program of healing meditation. When I saw her next, the hostility that had covered shame, had been replaced by a gentleness and strength that drew from the wellsprings of her being.

Loved Deep Within

How much useless energy is spent digging for painful memories, when the real hunger is for loving affirmation that allows the hurt we cannot access with all our searching and willing, to come to the surface. The deeper reaches of our psyche won't let go of the tightly clung to hurt, the deepest memories until confronted with love and nurture strong enough to replace the hurt. Then, the inward parts of us that clutch so tightly to pain begin to trust and let go.

So many of the prayer experiences we use in this book and on our retreats are designed to feed our deeper selves with affirmations; affirmations of God's love, affirmations of the essential wholeness of each one of us. The prayer experiences instill hope. But not the shallow kind of hope that suggests we can avoid reality by thinking "nice" thoughts. The prayer experiences bring hope by filling the inner recesses of our being with the central reality of faith — that we are created by a loving God who sent His Son to redeem us. We are grasped by God's affirmation. We experience His love at the very heart of things, a love that cannot and will not let us go. And that love makes all things fresh and new.

When we open our hearts wide to God's caring. The deeper roots of our nature find the permanent soil of an infinite love. We find in the cellar of our souls an ocean of infinite rest which gives meaning to our seemingly endless activities. There is a place within where the sea is always calm and the boats are steady, and Christian meditation takes our awareness to that place. The Kingdom of God, Jesus said, is within us.

When we enter into depth prayer we are taken into the arms of a God who will never forsake us from His embrace. As we surrender ourselves to the power of another, to something greater than ourselves, a force is mobilized within that helps affirm our goodness and wholeness.

Yet many of us fear this opening to love. We know that as we relax our guard and let love in we will feel the hurts we spend so much energy trying not to feel, and we fear these feelings will overwhelm us. But like Kate, and like so many I have known, when our guard relaxes because love has touched us, it goes down at just the right pace. Our pain didn't come in an instant, our healing doesn't come in an instant. Real and lasting healing resembles the gentle and gradual changing of seasons, rather than an overpowering summer thunderstorm.

We may never discover the origin of some of our pain, and that's o.k. We don't always need to know where it came from to let go of it. Romans 8 tells us that when we do not know how to pray, the Spirit prays through us with sighs too deep for words. Each of us is a fathomless depth and only God can know us fully. In meditation we give the Holy Spirit permission to search those depths. As our healing unfolds, we will find that at times a hurt is welling up inside of us and we don't know why. When that happens, we can grieve and weep and let go of our grip. This, is what I believe Paul meant, by sighs too deep for words.

Over a period of time, as prayer deepens the work of healing in our lives, a deep joy will root itself in the wellsprings of our being. The sunshine will appear to have more splendor and we shall be able to feel the warmth of words expressed by others rather than suspect ill will hidden in them. We learn to drink in the beauty of each present moment. The trees, the stars and blue hills, the touch of another human, appear to us as symbols aching with a meaning that can never be uttered in words. Nature begins to reflect the eternal. Water does more than wash our limbs, it brightens our hearts. The earth we walk on, does more than hold our bodies, it gladdens our minds, transmitting to our being the maternal tenderness of God.

CHAPTER TWO

What Is Healing Meditation?

How can I draw close to God? This is a question that all of us ask. At times it throbs like a toothache. At other times it lies buried beneath the clutter of everyday busyness. But the question remains always with us.

We yearn to draw close to God because there have been special grace-filled times in all of our lives when the mysterious at-homeness of His love caressed and enveloped us. Such times usually sneak up on us unexpectedly. Perhaps you are running along the beach. You cease to be aware of the movement of your muscles, or the splashing of your feet in the sand. The sound of the breaking waves stills and calms your mind. You seem one with the sea, the beach, you feel connected. Your fears leave you for a moment. You do not think of God, you experience Him. He seems closer to you than the blood cells that surge through your veins. From the cellar of your soul you call Him "Father".

Or perhaps such a "close encounter" comes as you tenderly touch and reverence the skin of your spouse, in the midst of the marriage kiss, maybe in the unexpected sense of love and peace you feel in the midst of tragedy, when the person you thought would never leave you, lies in a cool, metal box, awaiting burial.

Such times come in traditional ways too; while you are reading the Bible, receiving communion or voicing your praise.

These times tantalize us, tease us, make us hungry for more. They put us in touch with dimensions of our life that are missing; parts of ourselves we know were there all along, but had lost contact with.

This book presents practical pathways to growing close to God and becoming whole, ways so simple and so obvious that we easily overlook them. Learning Christian meditation will be an adventure, the adventure of discovering who you really are and loving who you really are. And as you more and more open your heart to the love of God in meditation, you will more and more learn to love the people around you. A fresh joy will root itself deep in the cellar of your soul. And as the new love and life within you help you to spend yourself for God, others and the poor, you can begin to say with St. Paul "It is not I who live but Christ who lives within me."

Opening Doors

Some things defy easy definition. No one definition or even a thousand definitions come close to describing God or love or hope. We sing, tell stories, paint pictures with words to get at realities that are larger than life.

So it is with meditation. In working on this book I searched for a word-picture, story, or image that would describe meditation. I ran scores of images through the slide-projector of my mind. I couldn't find one that by itself would convey the reality of meditation. I soon found that a number of different metaphors are needed.

One especially vivid picture description is based around an early memory. My mind returned to the simple, white-stucco house my Cherokee grandparents rented from the cotton mill they worked for. The first thing I saw every time I entered their tiny living room was a faded and sentiment-filled picture of Jesus, a staff in hand, knocking on the door of a house. The door was special; it had no outside latch. Under the picture there was a written explanation that told why. The note said that Jesus stood at the door of our hearts knocking, but that He would not barge in or open the door Himself. He was gentle; He respected our freedom. He wanted to be invited in. The latch was on the inside of our hearts. We could decide to let Him in. The picture quoted the words of the King James Bible: "Behold, I stand at the door and knock. If any man hear my voice and open up to me, I will come in and sup with him and he with me."

For me, this old painting is an apt description of Christian medita-

8.

tion. In Christian meditation we unlatch the doors of our hearts so Christ can fill us with His Gospel and His love.

And we open the door to Him not once but countless times. Our hearts have many doors and many rooms. The art of Christian meditation is the art of learning to open those doors to the endless beauty of our Eternal Lover.

Meditation is prayer that sinks below the surface of conscious thought. This is much of what is meant by the phrase "Praying with our whole hearts."

The concept of the subconcious is a concept accepted by almost everyone today. Our minds are often compared to icebergs. Only the smaller part of an iceberg protrudes above the surface. So it is with our consciousness; the larger part, the real us, lies below the surface. Here are stored old memories, good and bad, the fresh bright wonderful memories of early childhood and traumas buried so deep we wall them off from awareness. Here resides our sexuality. Here is the buried sublimity of our higher self as well as the cesspool of our darkness. Meditation is letting prayer sink to these hidden parts.

The Scriptures speak of these depths. "For the inward heart and mind of man are deep." Psalm 64B "The Lord is able to know man's deepest being; He reads man's heart ... " God does not see as man sees; man looks at appearances but Yahweh looks at the heart." (1 Sam. 16:7) He searches every heart and knows every plan that man devises" (I Chron. 28:9)

A motivational researcher summed up this need for the transformation of our subconscious: "If your faith is grounded in the subconscious mind, it will sustain you through any crisis. If it is no deeper than your conscious mind, it will desert you in the moment you are off guard. Its God-given power is amazing. Jesus Christ knew all about the subconscious mind and the part it played in our lives."

Despite the profound interest our modern culture has developed recently for meditation, we are an outward-turned, extroverted culture. We are not at home with inner silence, with our inner selves. That is why we run from solitude as quickly as we run from a mugger. Yet when we open the inner doors to God's unfathomable love, we find healing for our deepest wounds and the release of a whirlwind of strength for creative loving and creative living.

9.

How easy it is for our prayer to stay on the surface. Surface prayer is more like dictation than conversation. It tends to be a one-way monologue. We tell God what we want Him to do, ask Him to bless our plans and then go merrily on our way.

St. Catherine of Sienna, that feisty, fiery, loving woman of prayer who lived in the fourteenth century summed up this attitude. She was once asked why God no longer conversed with people in the familiar personal way He did in times past. She answered saying "God is no longer as personal as He once was because instead of treating Him as the Master and seeing ourselves as the disciple, we treat Him as the disciple and act like we are the Master."

In short, instead of praying, "Speak Lord, your servant is listening," we pray "Listen Lord, your servant is speaking."

The Special Difference

Meditation gets top billing today. Even some corporations have set aside special meditation rooms for their top executives. They hope this will help them avoid heart attacks. Meditation is in. Meditation lowers blood pressure, prevents disease, reduces stress, helps your sex life and improves your golf score. So the talk shows and popular magazines tell us.

And they are right. Secular meditation does bring some of these benefits. So does Christian meditation.

What, then, makes Christian meditation different?

Love! That's what makes the difference. The core of Christian meditation is love. Loving God, loving yourself, loving people, loving the whole world. As Augustine put it, "True, whole prayer is nothing but love."

Christian meditation at its heart is not just a great set of benefits. Yes, the benefits are there but they are secondary. All Christian prayer goes beyond the category of usefulness, beyond an enhanced ability to play a better tennis game or get more out of jogging.

It offers nothing less than a fiery and eternal love affair with the passionate and all-compassionate Lover who dances throughout the Cosmos and in the bosom of our own hearts. Christianity stands under the shadow of a Personal God. We believe in a God who cares, who is active in the world, the Yahweh who weaves His way throughout the story of ancient Israel, the story of Jesus. And the personal stories of each one of us.

Meditation is a powerful interchange of love with Him in the cellar of our souls. It is as St. Bonaventure so strikingly put it "the fire that totally inflames us and carries us into God ..." til we become "inflamed in the very marrow by the fire of the Holy Spirit."

In Christian meditation, we open up the inner passageways of our core being and allow this Passionate One of Israel, the God of Jesus, to express His love to us.

All prayer, all meditation begins with God's action toward us. Meditation is taking a sunbath in His caring, "an inner bath of love into which the soul plunges itself," as St. John Vianney put it. In meditation we allow Him to love us.

The Whole of Us

Christianity is the earthiest religion. It takes this world very seriously. "God so loved the world that He gave His only Son."

There is no special spiritual section inside us barricaded from the rest of us. God wants to involve each particle of our being, down to the cells in our fingernails in our love affair with Him.

So Christian meditation involves not just our religious side. Our sexuality, our bodies, our intellects, our relationships with others, our work, all become part of our meditation.

It is not so much that we pray as that we *become* a prayer. Early biographer of St. Francis, Thomas Celano, describes how Francis gave His whole self over to God in prayer: "All his attention and affection he directed with his *whole being* ... to the Lord, not so much praying as becoming himself a prayer." So it should be with us.

This book will carry you on a journey into meditation. Some of the themes of the prayer experiences may at first not seem particularly religious. They include personal relationships, the healing of past hurts, learning how to love. This is because God is concerned with all of us and when we pray, when we meditate, we present all of ourselves to Him.

The journey deeper into God's love hurts. It is not just a fresh high. In falling in love with anyone there is pain. We go through a healing process in meditation. We open up the different rooms

11.

of our heart to Christ and He sweeps them clean, then gets out the mop and scrubs away the encrusted grime. So there are times we must look at the grime and together with God take care of it. This is no lark. Facing the grunge inside of us hurts. Nikos Kazansakis describes this decision to yield to God's cleansing healing therapy: "God is fire and you must walk on it ... dance on it. At that moment the fire will become cool water. But until you reach that point, what a struggle, my Lord, what agony!"

Loving What God Loves

Francis of Assisi once said, years after he had been into his meditative journey that the things he formerly dispised were now sweet to him and the things he once loved he now disliked.

When you fall in love with someone, your likes begin to change. You begin to love the things they love. We first of all begin to love other Christians. "We know that we have passed from death to life when we begin to love other Christians," says the New Testament. We realize that we are on this journey with others — with friends ... with family ... with the Church.

Meditation is not a solitary, introspective, belly-gazing experience. It means an ongoing involvement with brothers and sisters.

There is an outward movement in meditation as well as an inward movement. We begin to love and serve the poor as Jesus loves and serves the poor. We become deeply involved in living out our love relationship in everyday life — loving God in those around us. We realize that the whole of the Cosmos groans, like us, for completion.

CHAPTER THREE

Imagination - A Doorway
To The Heart

A research project of the great psychoanalyst, Carl Jung, took him to the American Southwest, where he interviewed the famous Pueblo chief, Ochwraybiano. The doctor asked the Indian what he thought of white men. "Not much," replied the chief. "They're always restless, upset, looking for something more. That's why their faces are wrinkled."

He went on to say that white people must be crazy because they think with their heads: "And only crazy people think with their heads." "Then how do the Indians think?" asked Jung. "With their hearts, of course," answered the old chief.

One of the greatest tragedies of modern culture is that we think mostly with our heads. We leave out our heart, our inner core. As a result, our world is fragmented, partial; things just don't come "together", to use a modern phrase. Meditation, in a large part, means learning to think, to pray, to experience again with our hearts. We don't abandon thinking with our head, we bring head and heart together. We become whole.

How do you begin to pray, to think with the heart? You begin by using the language of the heart, the language of imagination. Modern psychologists and scientists are rediscovering what many of the more "together" cultures before us knew instinctively — that the language of the subconscious is the language of images, symbols, imagination.

A highly regarded researcher, Francis E. Long, of the California Institute of Transpersonal Psychology, sums this up:

> Imagery is the universal language of the unconscious. Thinking in pictures precedes thinking in words. Imagery is associated with direct perception and conveys in an instant feelings and observations which would take many words to describe.

Imagination - The Language of Scripture

This explains why the language of Scripture is full of imagery, symbolism, story. The Scriptures speak to the whole person, both head and heart, and therefore they are filled with the language of the imagination. They speak of God with such evocative imagery that they usher us into His presence. Amos Wilder, a highly respected Biblical scholar, thinks that the use of imagination is the dominant characteristic in the message of Jesus: "The hearer not only learns about that reality, he participates in it. He is invaded by it. ... Jesus' speech had the character not of instruction and ideas but of *compelling imagination*, a spell, ... a transformation."

Just look at some of the images Jesus used: A candle covered by a bushel basket, pearls thrown before swine, a treasure in a field, fishermen with a dragnet pulling in unimaginable varieties of fish, digging up treasure in a field.

Head and Heart Belong Together

I think it's important here to talk about some of the differences in "head" thinking and "heart" thinking. Because heart thinking has been neglected and plays such a vital role in our becoming whole doesn't mean that we should neglect rational thinking. To be complete we need to use both ways of experiencing the world. We need to blend head and heart together.

Most of us are used to rational thinking, linear logical thinking.

Many researchers associate rational, logical thinking with the left side of the brain. Intuitive, imaginative, creative thinking are centered in the right side of the brain.

As one friend put it: "With the logical part of us we comprehend and understand ideas about God; with the intuitive part of us we apprehend and experience Him."

In her best selling book, **Directing the Movies of Your Mind,** Adelaide Bry uses a striking illustration that shows the difference in the two ways of thinking. A freight train passes rapidly down the track and there are two people watching it. One person stands three feet from the track facing the train as it goes by. As the train goes by, all he sees is what is passing directly in front of him — the engine, one car at a time and then the caboose. This is much how the logical side of our brain operates — taking one thing at a time. Now let's imagine another person. This person looks at the train high above it, floating in a balloon. He can see all of the train at once. Instead of seeing one car or one part of a car at a time, he sees the total train, as well as the surrounding countryside. This is "holistic" experiencing, experiencing that takes in the whole.

Imaginative thinking is non-rational. This doesn't mean irrational. It means that it goes beyond the rational, penetrates deeper than the rational. What we are saying, in short, is that the old saying, "a picture is worth a thousand words" is profoundly true.

Phrases from Scripture such as, "The Word became a human being and dwelt among us," or "I am the Light of the World," do not make strict logical sense. They are non-rational, yet they convey realities and truth a thousand books could not convey. These are examples of powerful "holistic" thinking. They take us high in a hot air balloon and let us see the whole landscape in one glance.

Imagination, a Forgotten Art

Our modern society has lost touch with how to use the imagination. And it's killing us. Imagination once functioned as a means of evoking religious experience. Words conveyed pictures that would evoke the experience of God. In the last centuries we have lived in an abstract and labelled world, a world in which words no longer have the same ability to usher us into experience. This bleaches us of much of our humanity. This bleaches us of much of our ability to experience God.

Startling Discoveries

Physicians and researchers are finding bright new horizons in the healing of people's bodies and psyches through the use of relaxation and imagination. Case after case, study after study show that this powerful quote from psychotherapist Adelaide Bry, is profoundly true: "At a practical level, visualization has an uncanny ability to improve the quality of our lives. It does this through its power to heal the body and spirit, to reconstruct the past, and to reveal our hidden truths. . .the most dramatic visualizations touch the deepest part of ourselves, our essence, our core - and allow us to experience connections beyond ourselves." (**Directing the Movies of Your Mind,** Harper and Row) Pain control centers such as the UCLA Pain Control Center directed by Dr. David E. Bressler and the Health Rehabilitation Center in Wisconsin directed by Dr. C. Norman Shealy, founder of the Pain and Health Rehabilitation Center in LaCrosse, Wisconsin, are pioneering new directions. Patients come to these centers, often with migraine headaches or pain from back injuries that no amount of sedation will cure or relieve. By use of a combination of relaxation, imagination and meditation, Dr. Shealy has found that 72 percent of his patients have at least 50 percent improvement, and of those, at least half experience from 90 to 100 percent relief.

Imagination has a profound healing effect not only on the body but on the emotions as well. Dr. David Schultz, at the Westhaven VA Hospital in Connecticut, obtained some remarkable results with depressed patients. He divided depressed patients at these hospitals into two groups. One group he encouraged to use positive fantasies, positive daydreams, such as picturing themselves in a beautiful field or receiving compliments from someone who admired them. The other group was just encouraged to let daydreams come as they would without directing them or handling them in any way. Those directed into fantasies of beautiful nature scenes and of people affirming them

16.

showed remarkable improvement in their depression. Dr. Schultz later tried these methods with normal individuals and found that nature scenes and other healing images helped improve their moods when they were depressed and blue. Numerous other counselors have had excellent results helping normal people cope better with life and better fulfill their potential. All this points to the powerful impact our imaginations have upon both our emotions and bodies.

The experience of physicians and researchers in using the imagination to heal is simply rediscovery of what the writers of Scripture and many of the great figures of Christian tradition knew all along. Christian use of the imagination in prayer can carry us even further than these modern psychotherapeutic rediscoveries. "Grace," St. Thomas says, "builds upon the natural." Christian use of the imagination can put us in touch with God, the God of love whose touch brings wholeness.

CHAPTER FOUR

Imagination - A Way of Prayer

The three of us were on our way to Southern Louisiana "Cajun" country to conduct two weeks of retreats and seminars. As our little Datsun churned its way through the icy February rain, the center of my chest ached with anxiety and apprehension. I felt inadequate — physically, emotionally, and spiritually for the tasks that awaited me in Louisiana.

Several weeks earlier in an emergency operation, a surgeon took out my infected, pus-filled gallbladder that was about to burst. The operation saved my life.

I was really not ready for such an exhausting mission and the doctor had only reluctantly given me permission for the trip.

The day we set our, my winter cold turned into a nasty bronchitis. I was in such a haze from my physical condition that putting two coherent sentences together took effort. Pictures of my stammering in front of the audiences passed through my mind. I had no idea what I was going to say.

The first engagement concerned me the most. I was supposed to lead a day of recollection for a group of 400 young people aged thirteen through twenty-three from Lafayette diocesan youth groups.

One of my co-workers, Pat Bartholomew, a young man whose eyes glisten with vitality and determination picked up the worry in my face. With half a smile he said, "Eddie, here's a time I can remind you of some of the advice you give to other people. God can use you most when you are at your weakest. You've been telling people lately how by using the imagination in prayer we can become channels for God's love. Here's a time for you to try it."

I took up his challenge. My hazy mind began to go over scenes in Scripture that involve healing light imagery. My mind turned to the lowly young girl, Mary, who opened her heart wide enough to receive the light of God at the annunciation. I remembered the scene of James and John standing in awe at the light of the transfiguration and Saul knocked off his horse by the blinding light of God's presence.

I visualized a large ray of soothing healing light shining, beaming down on me as I sat in the little Datsun seat. I allowed that light to energize me, comfort me, heal me, and tell me of God's love in a way deeper than words. Every time my mind wandered away I returned to the image of myself sitting under the light of God's Presence.

That night as I lay in bed awaiting sleep the picture prayer changed. The light not only surrounded me but went through my hands and heart. It went out from me and surrounded others. I pictured the whole gym full of young people inundated in the light of God's love.

The next day with the 400 young people became the bright spot of our whole year of retreats. I don't remember what I said. My mind was still foggy; my chest still ached. But I felt a great love from beyond myself surge through me as I spoke. I remember leading them through some of the meditations I used in my own prayer. By the end of the day many were in tears, they were so deeply touched. A score or more asked to take the microphone and briefly share a little of what had happened in their hearts that day. Some as young as thirteen told how their faith became alive for them for the first time. One muscular young man of twenty, a former linebacker for LSU who had dropped out of football because of a knee injury, came forward. His eyes moist with tears he told how he had been afraid to be weak and transparent. That day he had learned the power of not pretending. He said he wanted his friends to be Christian friends; he was choosing a Christian lifestyle.

As I drove away that evening I was reconvinced that God works best through our weakness. But in a way that goes beyond just the natural, it also enabled more of me to become a channel of a light and a healing love that was beyond myself. I was saying a yes with my subconscious as well as my conscious mind.

19.

Programmed Imagination in Prayer

Programmed imagination in prayer is when we actively set up certain scenes to imagine. The symbols, the stories, the images of Scripture, provide hundreds of starting-off places. Such visualizations help deepen our sense of God's loving us. Such active imagination is dosing ourselves with the Gospel. We begin to center our personalities around Gospel symbols and Gospel pictures. We open doors for God's message of love in the bosom of our souls.

Recently I had a great deal of difficulty working on some of my writing projects. I had a classic case of writer's block. Sitting at the typewriter and staring at a blank page every day took big chunks out of my self-image. Then I began to let it be a matter of prayer. I thanked God for His love for me. I told Him that I recognized that He loved me whether I worked on my book project and articles or not. Then I said, "Lord, I know you have called me to write. Help me with my writing."

I pictured finished manuscripts. I pictured myself thumbing through the pages while surrounded by the light of God's love. I imagined some of my friends saying, "This material really touched me to the heart. It really helped me love the poor; it helped put me in contact with God." Then I saw myself doing the tasks that were involved in writing — taking notes, typing, dictating.

There was no overnight miracle. But I daily used this picture prayer when I asked God to help me with my writing. Such prayer bolstered and strengthened my inner self. The energies and abilities found deep in me were marshalled to the task before me. It took several weeks, but then I suddenly found myself flooded with ideas. The discipline that had seemed so hard now seemed easy. I organized my tasks daily and the material began to pour out. I finished pages a day rather than just a few paragraphs. Many who read the material were touched. I had experienced the power of picture prayer.

Robert, a member of my tiny community who has a profound, simple spirituality, wanted so much for his life to be in touch with the poor. Although we live a simple lifestyle in a poor neighborhood, we were invited to speak all over the world and the people who invite us take us to the fanciest restaurants, the nicest clubs, the nicest beaches. And living a life of simplicity and poverty was important for us at that time. And because a large part of our apostlate is reaching out, helping to renew parishes and give retreats, we are not home all year round in order to develop a steady ministry to the poor. We knew we needed the poor in our lives not just for their sakes, but for ours. We needed the grace of God that comes through the poor, because the poor are so close to Him.

Robert especially began to pray daily that God would help him in knowing how to love the poor and let the poor love him. He prayed the Scripture with his imagination, "Inasmuch as You have done it to the least of these, my brethern, you have done it unto Me."

He pictured himself loving and being loved by different types of poor people. Then, after weeks fo this, some of our elderly neighbors, some on food stamps, one who had a severe debilitating stroke, another had his wife die, began to come to us spontaneously, just to be around us. Robert especially took time for them, sitting with them on the porch, taking them to lunch, taking them for rides, just being someone to help take away their loneliness.

He found an old man whose income was $200 a month social security, gathering aluminum cans from trash cans in the park. Then he started having lunch with him. He spends a great deal of time with friends like these whose need is obvious. And they have been a great joy to him and God's love has come to him in such beautiful ways through them. His picture prayer brought him into contact with the poor. His picture prayer helped him begin to live the gospel. Most of us don't have the same intense vocation to be involved with the poor that Robert has. But each of us according to our own calling in life can use imagination prayer to bolster our decision to live the Gospels in our own life situation.

Gospel Commercials

Imaginative prayer is a window to self-knowledge.

In imagination we can dose ourselves with Gospel commercials. Commercials on television, radio, and in the movies know this technique of imagination. I know of some car commercials that have powerful, cosmic, magical religious symbolism as well as sexy girls, all pointing out the wonders of some new sports car. They know the route to the core of us. These commercials tell us that our salvation, our wholeness, comes in consuming and buying more and more. They lie to us.

To counteract their muddy, murky message we need to give ourselves daily Gospel commercials. We need to take the truths and power of the messages of Scripture and Christian Tradition and use them to fill our inner selves with powerful and strengthening images. We need images that heal us and help us to know the power of God's love, help us to open the deepest doors of our heart to the penetrating light of that love. They help us to know that we are like the baby in our Father's arms, to help us to know His caresses, His loving caring, His tenderness. They lead us to spend ourselves in serving and loving others. We begin to integrate our personalities around these images.

Imagination Prayer and Scriptures

The Scriptures are a great textbook on prayer, expecially the Psalms and Canticles. They often show an intimate picture of the prayer lives of many people. This is especially true of the Psalmists. Imagination played an important role in the personal prayer of Psalmists.

The next time you have your Bible out, just thumb through the Psalms. Look at how many powerful picture images are painted by the authors. Look at the powerful visualizations that the writers use in their prayer such as this powerful image quoted from 2 Sam. 22:1-7: "The waves of death was around me. The waves of destruction rolled over me. . ." "In my trouble I called to the Lord; I called to my God for help. The Lord reached down from above and took hold of me; He pulled me out of the deep waters."

The 23rd Psalm is an outstanding example of imaginative prayer.

The Age of Faith, that high point of Christian experience from 1050 to 1350, was a time of wonder, a time of imagination. This was the time that produced the great cathedrals. Christian art, Christian music, all helped the use of the imagination. The great cathedrals such as Chartres, Notre Dame, have been called picture Bibles because of their very construction, their window paintings, vault of heaven, powerfully stimulated the imagination.

22.

The builder of the first Gothic Church, Abbott Suger, gives us some powerful insight into the power of imagination and prayer. He describes how he felt on entering the first Gothic church building in 1144. The colored glass construction of the church, he said, had a powerful ability to transform "that which is material to that which is immaterial. . .then it seems to me that I see myself dwelling, as it were, in some strange region of the universe which neither exists entirely in the slime of earth nor entirely in the purity of heaven; and that, by the grace of God, I can be transported from the inferior to that higher world."

So many things that are a part of Christianity today are meant to have the same effect upon our prayer as the visualizations of the writers of Scripture and the builders of the Cathedrals. The eucharistic service is a drama, an acting out, an imagination. Church buildings, church windows, hymns, full as they are of images, also have this effect. Sadly, we have forgotten how to use our imaginations. We have forgottend the power of the non-rational. As Carl Jung put it, "we are, indeed the rightful heirs of Christian symbolism, but this inheritance we have somehow squandered."

Guided Prayer Experiences

The prayer experiences in this book may seem like a new modern way of praying to you.

Actually, the prayer experiences or guided meditations contained here are simply modern expressions of very ancient ways of praying.

The 23rd Psalm puts the listener into a green pasture, carries him through a valley, lets oil stream down his head and has him picture God as shepherd.

The Hebrews often recited psalms to the stilling relaxing music of the lyre. The listener was deeply relaxed by the music and stilling words, and filled with healing, spiritual imagery.

The chant of the early Church had a remarkable soothing relaxing quality. The words, either from Scripture or based on Scripture, filled these early Christians with the imagery of the faith.

Specific meditations or poems, usually read to the background of soft music were also composed.

One of the greatest composers of such "guided prayer experiences" was St. Paulinus of Nola, a married bishop who lived in the fourth century. Here are some parts of one of his image-filled poems that lead the listener into prayer.

"Lighten yourselves in preparation for Christ, and being now relieved of your burdensome luggage, free your feet of its bonds. Become naked in this world to be clothed in abundance of light. . .May the clouds which transport saints readily bear you in their unsubstantial grasp. . .And may God steep you in His brightness that the shining glory of eternal life may draw your mortality within it."

Paulinus "meditations" were read to groups of people with a gentle musical background. St. Bonaventure, the first great Franciscan scholar who lived in the thirteenth century, wrote guided meditations that were typical of many other authors during his period. His book **The Tree of Life**, is essentially a long guided prayer experience that carries the listener or reader into depth prayer through the use of imagery. He calls fourth all of the senses. Here are some brief excerpts that give a taste of what the whole book is like. Writing of the light of the annunciation, he says:

"Oh, if you could feel in some way the quality and intensity of that fire sent from heaven, the refreshing coolness that accompanied it, the consolation it imparted. . ." (p. 127.)
(The Works of Bonaventure, Paulist)

In the section of the meditation that deals with Jesus' birth, he says:

". . .embrace that divine manager; press your lips upon and kiss the boy's feet. Then in your mind keep the shepherd's watch. . ." (p. 129). "Receive the infant in your arms" (p. 131). **(The Works of Bonaventure,** Paulist)

Many of the hymns of the evangelical hymn writers create much the same type prayer experience. Imagery and music blend together to reach the believers inner core with the power of the Gospel.

In a hymn: Charles Wesley, the co-founder of the Methodist Movement wrote:

"The light of life eternal darts into our souls a dazzling ray, a drop of heaven overflows our hearts, and deluges the house of clay."

The prayer experiences in this book are inspired by this old tradition of guided Christian imagery. They put that imagery in today's language, in today's forms, but the roots of such prayer experiences are ancient.

CHAPTER FIVE
How To Do It:
It's Easier Than You Think

The fact that you have read this far indicates you are interested in learning how to meditate. You sense that new and fresh dimensions of living and loving can open up to you.

But you may also be frightened. Whenever we start something new, especially something that involves us so totally as meditation, we fear we will fail.

For most of us, especially the most "successful" of us, our lives have held many series of obstacle courses - school, job-hunting, dating, etc. Fear of failure has been a constant companion in so many of life's endeavors. So as you begin to deepen your prayer you are probably asking: "Is this something else I might fail at?"

I have some shocking and refreshing news for you - it is impossible to try to pray and fail! Just as it is impossible to try to love God and fail. Trying to love God is loving Him and trying to pray is praying.

Imagine a group of office workers gathering around the coffee pot at break time. They talk about their toddlers, their young children. The smallest little action a young child takes to show love to parents bring great delight to their heart. A color drawing with purple grass given to mother makes her heart leap, no matter that the grass is a purple streak and the sky smudgy yellow.

You would never see this group of office workers say "My little girl tried to love me with a picture but drew it messy so she failed in loving me."

No, the slightest most muddled action of a young child to express love to a parent usually brings joy, just as the first mutters that sound like "Mama" or Daddy" bring delight.

So it is with God. Our slightest effort as His children to love Him in prayer causes His heart to leap. As St. Theophan the Recluse puts it: "Take one feeble step toward God and He will take a thousand toward you."

Trying to pray is praying — You cannot fail!

No matter how boring, how dry, or how distracted or how reluctant your quiet time may be, your prayer, your meditation, reaches beyond the heavens.

When and Where

The first and only commandment in meditation is to relax. This is truly a "let go and let God" type of prayer. We get out of the driver's seat and let Him in.

It is usually helpful to wait two hours after a heavy meal and one hour after a substaintial snack. It is hard to pray deeply when our body is actively involved in digestion. Also, don't pick your sleepiest time to pray.

The place should be as quiet and as private as possible but if you have a house full children and pets, the Lord understands, and will give you grace in any situation.

Begin, either before or after you have relaxed, to talk to God as a friend. Tell Him what is going on in you, thank Him, and be personal. Give yourself over to Him for the period of meditation you you are about to begin. Ask Him to do with you what He wills. A good prayer of abandonment is to simply say, "Father into Your hands I commend my spirit".

Don't kneel for meditative prayer. Kneeling at other times is fine, but if you kneel for mediation your mind will be on your aching knees and not on resting in God. Sitting in a chair that is not too hard and not too soft is usually the best position. Keep your spine relatively straight, but not rigid. Lying on the floor especially on your back is a great position that keeps the itches and twitches of your body from bothering you. The drawback is that many tend to go to sleep in this position, especially early in the morning. If this is your problem then this position is not for you.

The Shocking News About
Wandering Thoughts

Here you are in your chair; you have given yourself to God in
your prayer and started your meditation. Then, after a few minutes,
suddenly you realize you have wandered from what you were
meditating on.

You are thinking about the pizza you are going to have for supper
or the spat you just had with a neighbor. Here is where wandering
thoughts come in, and here it is that many think they have failed
at prayer.

I have some shocking information for you. We all have wandering thoughts in our prayer. I'm fairly certain Jesus did. He was human
and human beings have busy "attics". Wandering thoughts, no matter what they are, are to be expected. This haze of thoughts was
with us all along, buried deep within us, with a good strong cork
stopping up the bottle. They were there unnoticed causing irritability,
high blood pressure and fatigue. In meditation, you allow God to
uncork you and a parade of cloudy images and thoughts marches by.

The reason this takes place is because you are being emptied out.
Celano said of St. Francis' prayer times that "he made room for Jesus
Christ in the inner recesses of his heart". Letting this stream of
thoughts parade by us and then out of us empties us so that there
is more room inside for God. The good news is that wandering
thoughts don't mean failure; they are part of the process.

Don't try to fight wandering thoughts or you will be like Brer rab-
bit fighting the tar baby. The more you fight the more you get stuck
in the tar. You gave yourself to God for your prayer time and what
happens to you during it is His business. You did not will to have
wandering thoughts. It happened to you before you noticed it. Fr.
William Menninger, the Cistercian father who teaches contemplative prayer, has a fantastic thought on this. He says, "If in
the midst of your thirty minute prayer time, you stop your prayer
a hundred times and have to return to it a hundred times, you have
made one hundred separate acts of loving God." When you realize
your mind has wandered, gently return to your prayer. Slightly prefer
your prayer phrase to your wandering thoughts and images.

"Holy Drowsiness"

There is more shocking good news about prayer. Sleepiness doesn't mean failure. Many contemplatives of the tradition speak of the sleep of contemplation. "I sleep but my soul it keeps watch," said St. Bernard of Clairveaux. "Contemplative prayer is a resting, a resting in the arms of our Father. Most of us get sleepy when we rest..."

Many of the mystical ascetical theologians speak of sleepiness as a sign of a deepening prayer life. St. Teresa of Avila called it "Holy Drowsiness." St. Francis DeSales said "I had rather be asleep on the breast of God than awake in any other place." This corresponds to what scientists say of meditative states. In meditation prayer you are often in "theta" state which is a state of restful alertness. People often feel sleepy in this state.

What if you actually fall hard asleep in prayer, the snoring type of sleep? First of all, a good preventive for this is to pray at your most awake times, get plenty of daily exercise, and enough sleep at night. Besides this, there is not much more you can do. You do not will to fall asleep. The last act of your will before you fall asleep is an act of loving God, so you fall asleep in His arms. As the great fourteenth century work on contemplation, **The Cloud of Unknowing**, says: "If in the midst of this work of love (contemplation) you should fall asleep, praise God." Well put!!

Tips on Using the Imagination in Prayer

Most of the meditations in this book call for some use of the imagination. When we were little, imagination came easy. We knew the language of imagination before we knew the language of words. But years of sitting six hours a day in hard school desks, usually bored, caused our imaginative ability to go limp, to atrophy.

Relaxation - The first step to using the imagination in your prayer time is to relax. Relaxation releases the ability to imagine. Exercises and suggestions in the following chapter can help you learn to relax.

We Experience the Imagination in Different Ways - Imagination is more than just seeing with our mind's eye. It involves all the senses - taste, touch, hearing, smell, the sense of body movement.

Some people are better at imagining certain senses than other senses. Some people rarely "see" or experience anything. Rather, they have a "sense" of the scene imagined without visualizing, hearing, or touching. Just having this "sense" of the scene to be imagined is just as powerful as those who have 3D technicolor imagination.

My own way of imagination is a mixture of "sensing" and seeing. I get fleeting glimpses only, of the scene to be imagined, but I have a real sense of being there.

Be at Home with Your Experience - Whatever your experience of imagination, learn to be at home with it. The more you actively practice imagination, the more acute your imagination will become.

Just as a television set that is picking up a distant station, we all have static and other bleeding in across the scene. A relaxed attitude about your imagination, whatever your experience, is the key to unlocking it. Remember, if you try, you can't fail. Even the slightest glimpse or sense of the scene to be imagined integrates us, opens us to God and helps us to become more whole.

How to Use the Prayer Experiences in this Book

The prayer experiences in this book are designed to gently guide you into depth prayer. Some you will take to immediately, others you might discover are not for your right now. You might return to them sometime later and find that they take on a new life.

Some will be special and you will return to them often and probably have a different experience each time.

All of them, hopefully, will help you learn to design and pray meditations that are uniquely your own.

Read over the special prayer experiences once or twice slowly. Then close your eyes, go through a period of relaxation and carry yourself through the experience. Don't worry about getting everything exactly right.

Praying with a Cassette

Another way of using the prayer experience is to gently, softly, and with many pauses, record them on cassette and play them back to yourself.

Pray them with others. Another variation is to use them with one or more friends. You can take turns guiding one another through the prayer experiences by slowly reading them to one another. This can be a great way to strengthen and build spiritual friendships.

Music

Certain instrumental music deeply relaxes you and unlocks the imagination. Certain classical pieces, especially certain baroque pieces have this ability. The last five years have also seen new compositions designed especially to deepen relaxation and meditation as well as release imaginative ability. You might want to try playing such music as background to your meditation.

CHAPTER SIX

Relaxation - Sinking Into Grace

Anxiety, worry, insomnia, irritability, heartburn, indigestion, headaches, high blood pressure. These and similar maladies are symptoms of a stressful existence. And how little most of us know about ways to relieve stress.

A bird sits on a tree branch. A cat curls up in the sunlit spot from a window. A dog lies on the grass, head between his paws. Animals know how to relax, naturally. But we busy humans have forgotten how to relax -- and it's killing us.

Relaxation, revitalizes us, renews us, gives us time to rejuvenate both physically and emotionally.

In Christian relaxation our being lets go in His love. As the Lutheran pastor Jacob Boeme of the seventeenth century put it, "We sink into the ground of His mercy." "His love is there and leads you from anxiety into God."

Relaxation is essential for imagination prayer. As Adelaide Bry puts it, "Letting go into relaxation is like dimming the lights in a movie theater. Both let you see the images on the screen."

Much of our tension is held within our muscles. Relaxing our muscles helps us let go of tension.

The following prayer-script with comforting Scripture is helpful in relaxing. Read it over several times slowly, then close your eyes and repeat the main ideas to yourself. You will quietly be telling the different parts of your body to relax. You will be amazed at the results.

Modern Psalm of Relaxation

Jesus took our care on himself.
His love is ease and calm, Shalom.
And we can relax and let go, relax
and let go, relax and let go in Him
Relaxed. Relaxed. Relaxed.
The whole of my body relaxed and calm
God's calmness and relaxation all through me
My face, my heart, my mind.
Shalom. Shalom. Shalom.
My legs, arms, whole body, are relaxed
by God's Shalom.
The muscles around my cheeks,
my mouth, are relaxed, deeply relaxed.
The relaxation flows to my lips,
tongue and throat.
Like a child resting in it's mother's arms
so is my heart stilled and calmed in God.
Like a child resting in it's mother's arms
so is my heart stilled and calmed in God.
Jesus wants me to relax.
Relax and let go,
resting my heart in Him.
Relaxed -- Relaxed -- Relaxed
All my muscles let go,
In my hands, arms, legs, and my
whole body, let go.
My neck, shoulders, and upper body
are loose and relaxed.
Deeper and deeper into the ease of God's love.
Deeper and deeper into prayer.
In my heart I say:
I let go -- I let go -- I let go
I let God -- I let God -- I let God
God's love is relaxing warmth all about me,
I rest in my Father's love,

I relax in His eternal cherishing.
Because of His love He takes my burdens and fears.
Anxiety, fear, and tension leave me.
Anxiety, fear, and tension leave me.
Anxiety, fear, and tension leave me.
His love is a sponge all around me
absorbing fear.
Nothing disturbs me, nothing alarms me,
The ease of His peace all through me.
His ease in my face,
His ease in my heart. His ease in my mind.
The quiet breath of His in my breath.
Breathing easily and deeply,
Breathing easily and deeply.
I am breathing easily and deeply,
easily and deeply,
easily and deeply,
because His love breathes in me.

Centering Prayer -- A Way of Relaxation

Centering prayer is an ancient and deeply stilling form of Christian prayer. Find a short prayer phrase that is meaningful to you such as "Abba, Father," "Lord Jesus, have Mercy," "Lord Jesus, Healer, heal me," or some other prayful phrase. Repeat the phrase silently. If you are distracted, gently return to your prayer phrase.

You will be surprised by how a few minutes of this prayer calms you and revitalizes you.

SECTION II

EXPERIENCING GOD'S LOVE

CHAPTER SEVEN

A Love That Changes Us

Time and time again, I see the change that takes place when people discover the love of the God made visible in Jesus.

My friend Billy's experience beautifully illustrates this. Billy is an ex-army officer in his early forties, an avid jogger and veteran of the Boston Marathon. He discovered meditation before he discovered Christ.

I met him with a glass of fruit punch in his hand at the home of mutual friends during a New Year's Eve party. My friends introduced us saying: "I know you two will have a lot in common. You're both interested in meditation." Meeting someone with such a similar interest, I became my overtalkative, excited self. I went on and on about Paul's understanding of love, the writings of Teresa of Avila, John and Charles Wesly. But I noticed something wasn't connecting. Billy's eyes kept moving up and down in little jerks. I knew it was time to shut up and let him speak.

After he talked a few minutes, I knew his experience of meditation was different from mine. Billy had been searching for inner pathways but had avoided Christian pathways.

The past few years had taken him on quite a journey. Many of the things he looked into were beneficial and valid in themselves. He had visited American Indian communities in the Southwest and talked to their spiritual masters. He had read meditation manuals and was in the midst of working on a graduate degree in counseling psychology. He experienced many techniques from Eastern religions. Yet, I sensed it was not all coming together for him. There seemed to be little integration. Things were not connecting.

He talked about the awesome power he believed our minds have to control our outer environment. It appeared that meditation for him was a set of methods he could use to control both his internal world and the very concrete external world outside him.

I didn't see Billy for another year. During that time he passed through stormy times. He and his wife separated. He changed jobs. He experienced his limits as a person. His techniques were not enough. He knew he was no longer in control either of his inside world or of his outside world. And he came in touch with the limitless love of God in Christ in Christianity. He made a decision to be baptized, confirmed and received into the church.

He came to see us at our house just after that decision. This strong man broke down and shook with sobs. Accepting his limits, willing to give up control was not an easy thing. Then it seemed day by day a change took place in him. Meditation, rather than being a means of control, now became a means of experiencing God's accepting love. An amazing personal integration, a new tenderness came to his personality. He began to form many close Christian friendships.

A year after his baptism he took over leadership of the parish youth group. It flourished. Many of his natural abilities blossomed. His problems didn't magically work themselves out; everything he has done had not been blessed with the Midas touch of success. but his walk, the look in his eye, the gentleness of his voice, tell of a deep ability to love himself that has come through accepting God's acceptance.

Incarnate Love Means Everyday Love

God is boundless love, an eternity of caring. As 1st John puts it: "God is love, and those who dwell in love dwell in God."

But just the statement "God is love", by itself is not enough. The consumer society that surrounds us too greatly influences our concept of love. And this popular view of love is as sticky sweet, as unstable and mushy, as tapioca pudding. Popular songs pound in the idea that love is being hooked on feelings.

For the statement "God is love" to catch our attention and change us; it must be fleshed out, become everyday, approachable, incarnate.

And this is exactly what happened in Jesus. In Him the endless ocean of love that is God became touchable, approachable, real. Infinite, ineffable love became an everyday love. From his earliest days, Jesus experienced a mysterious love all around Him and in the center of His being. At some point, in the most natural way, He began to call this love, "Abba", the Aramaic word for Daddy. This was the image that most fully expressed His relationship to that love. Later, He came to know the love he called "Daddy" was also His own innermost identity. Through the earthy, concrete stories He told, and through the story that was His life, He made that love real for us.

Jesus turned the world's understanding of things upside down. His Father loved with a scandalous love - the prostitutes, the drunkards, the tax collectors were special objects of His passionate caring. He was the shepherd that would leave the ninety-nine sheep for the one lost sheep. The father who embraced and kissed the returning son who had squandered all that the father had given him. He was the woman (yes, Jesus did compare God to a woman) who swept the house clean searching for the lost coin. And Jesus showed that searching love of God Himself by mingling with the prostitutes and drunkards, and even having people hurl at Him the accusation of being a glutton and drunkard. By the way He lived His life, He showed what God was like, reaching to people in the deepest level of their woundedness, loving the undeserving.

In the Gospel of John,, He unsettles His disciples' view of the order of things by becoming their servant — washing their feet. On the cross, His most ultimate giving of Himself, He shows the depths to which God goes to win us back and to heal our wounded hearts and our wounded world. And through His resurrection He promises a future in which this loving God will win out, will have the final say over the forces of dehumanization, destruction and fear that are part of the lives of each one of us, and part of the life our world.

Ordinary Love

The stories Jesus told and the story of His life are full of the earthy ordinary details of everyday life, the details of business, finances, farming, sickness, death.

And that's the world in which we live our lives, and God's love can come to us in this ordinary, everyday world. When I am filled with self doubt, when some of my projects have failed, when my stomach aches with disappointment, I need a God who loves me despite my seeming failure. I need a God who sees right past the layers of falsity and fear in my personality to the wonderful, unique creature that is the real me.

This experience of the mystery of His love helps be believe in myself again. And when I have hurt others, hurt God and hurt myself by running off my own way, He receives me back, kisses and embraces me, like the father who embraced the prodigal son.

I need the experience of this love every day in the little concrete events of my daily life. From spats I have with friends to frustrations over finances, He greets me with the good news that I am loved, accepted — and His love speeds me along my journey to wholeness.

His love is there to challenge me, every time when I decide to receive it. I know that it's risky business, because when I open my heart, my being, my everyday life to the God who loves like the God who reveals Himself through Jesus, I have no other choice but to struggle to love like that. Everytime I open myself up to that love, that love prods me on, challenges me to begin, even in some small measure, to love in the same way. I know that if I open myself to His love, I open myself to change. When I let Him hold me close I find that he needs me as much as I need Him, and this scares me. He needs me to be an agent of His peace. To weep with those who weep, to greet Him in "the least of those my brothers."

Barriers to Experiencing God's Love

The images at work, school and on T.V. that bombard us every day do not reinforce the idea that we are the children of a loving father who holds us tenderly in the palms of his hands. So if we wish to experience God's love we need to expose ourselves daily to the reality of that love and the reality of our daily need for that love.

Christian prayer, meditation, the eucharist, Scripture reflection, loving connections with other Christians, are all pathways we can open daily, pathways for the sunlight of God's love to reach the cellars of our being.

Another barrier is when we conceive of the experience of God only as an emotion. We think we're experiencing God's love only when we "feel" It. Yes, there will be times when our emotions vibrate like violin strings from the touch of His hand upon us. And such times should be graciously received for these are mountain-top experiences that help us see the whole of our lives. From high up we can see the whole countryside in perspective. But a life that moved from just one high to another would be an artificial life, an unreal life. We can experience His love even when we don't feel it; even if our feelings are as dry as the sands of the desert.

Marriage shows this clearly. How many times I have seen people transformed after they marry, especially when there is a strong loving marriage with open communication. One friend married several months ago for the first time. A new mellowness rooted itself in his personality. Overly masculine and controlled before, he began to approach life with a feminine tenderness along with his natural masculine strength. A source of fresh life welled up in him. The daily experience of someone special loving him, spending his time at home with someone who cherished him, instead of by himself, all had a steadying, healing, transforming effect on his personality. Yes, there were high and giddy times for him that showed in the brightness of his eyes. He also had his low moments, and his in-between moments.

Whatever his feelings, every week of his marriage, so it seems, has increased his ability to cherish and care about others. An increasing capacity to experience creation around him blossomed.

So it is with God. His love is no constant high. Rather, we open ourselves to the presence of one who steadily loves us. We flower, we look upon the world with a loving gaze. Compassion takes root deep within us. We have our painful times and our joyous times, but we go through the journey of our lives with the deepening knowledge that we go through that journey with the steadiness of the Eternal Lover beside us.

The Purpose of the Following Meditations

The following meditations are to help us to open our personalities even more to the experience of God's love. All prayer does this. Any type of prayer does this. The following meditations in this section and in the section that follows are especially designed to highlight our awareness that we stand in the presence of One who loves us. They bombard us with images and affirmations that help us open the cellar doors within us. These meditations are designed to help us allow the love of the Eternal Lover meet us in the stuff of daily living.

CHAPTER EIGHT

This Is Me, Lord, Right Now

One of the main reasons that prayer can feel artificial, unreal, is that we often hide our real feelings from ourselves and from God.

As T.S. Eliot put it: "We prepare a face to meet the faces that we meet." Hiding from others, God, and ourselves absorbs a great amount of emotional and physical energy and leaves us strained and tired. When we take time to notice and acknowledge our emotions, or how our body feels at the moment -- when we are honest -- the energy we tie up in repression can be used for more effective living and loving. Our whole being loosens up and relaxes. We are freed to be more present to the here and now. So many of the authors of the Scriptures had that honest awareness of themselves. When we acknowledge where we are at the moment, it's easier for God's love to penetrate us more deeply.

Noticing our feelings is different from being overwhelmed by them. It is one thing to fly into an uncontrolled rage and strike out at a friend or family member, and quite another to prayerfully acknowledge our emotions and say to ourself and to God: "I'm feeling intense anger right now."

Italian psychotherapist and author Roberto Assagioli, who incorporates so many ideas from Christian spiritual masters in his writings says "We are dominated by everything with which our self becomes identified. We can dominate and control everything from which we disidentify ourselves."

Frances E. Vaughn, in her book **Intuition**, (Doubleday) beautifully describes this process: "Thus you may be aware of having fear, for example, as part of the contents of consciousness, without becoming identified with it or controlled by it. Unlike repressed feelings, which distort perception, contribute to chronic tension, and distract one's attention from the present, emotions which are observed. . come and go and change naturally."

Prayer Experience
Coming as You are Before God's Love

Take time to relax and be still. Let your attention move over your body. Notice any tense or tight muscles. Notice any physical pain or discomfort. . . Become aware of the emotions you are feeling now... Feel them. . . What fears are your feeling?. . . What guilts?. . . What anger?. . . What joys are you feeling?. . . What feelings of affection?. . .

What are some of the thoughts your are thinking?. . . Don't judge or try to change what you are feeling or thinking. Just notice and acknowledge.

When you have noticed where you are right now, give yourself as you are, where you are, to God.

Pray this prayer or a similar prayer of your own:

"Here I am Lord. This is me right now. I place myself as I am before your all-caring and all-forgiving love. I open myself to your healing touch. I open myself to the unfathomable mystery of your Love. I allow you to love me."

Rest in silence several minutes in the sunlight of His love.

Pause in silence before God's Love.

CHAPTER NINE

The Gentle Strength of Remembering

How often my mind and heart return to my grandparent's one-bedroom cotton mill house.

I have learned as much about prayer and meditation from simple-hearted people like them than from all of the many scores of books on spirituality I have studied.

Brought up in the rough days following the Civil War by her dirt poor grandmother, my own grandmother, as a child, knew the daily threat to survival that people in Bangladesh and Calcutta live with today. She and her family would go for weeks with nothing to subsist on but moldy corn meal, and milk from an old cow. Illness, possible death of family members, and the threat of starvation constantly walked beside them. Those rough times made my grandmother strong, sweet, and steady rather than bitter. Their struggle knitted her and her family closely to one another and to God.

When she married, she and my Cherokee grandfather held stable mill jobs during hard times. The dinner table was usually filled with down and out relatives and acquaintances. A black family with several small children and no jobs or income, took their meals with my grandparents.

She didn't learn to read until after she had given birth to three children; but there was a wisdom and compassion in her bright eyes that gave evidence of a knowledge far deeper than could ever be contained in libraries.

So many of the times I spent with her as a child she would get out the bulky white family Bible, sit in the rocker by the corner and slowly read each word. Her eyes would be half closed and she would just drift off. I knew what she was doing; she was remembering. Remembering the closeness and warmth of her early days, all the people she had known; remembering the times that God had touched her in the midst of crisis, remembering those who had died.

As she went about her housework, the radio stayed on the country channel. From time to time they played the sentiment-filled Gospel song, "Precious Memories." "Precious memories, how they linger, how they satisfy my soul. . .in the stilllness of the twilight, precious sacred scenes unfold." Her eyes would become moist and she would lean on her broom, or take the iron off the clothes and set it upright for a moment, and drift. Her facial muscles would relax and an aura of peace and strenght would envelope her. These times of going back to the strengths of the past were much of the source of the beauty in my grandmother.

So many ways of praying are so obvious we miss them. Remembering can lead to the deepest meditative states. When we remember the special times God has blessed us, that strength becomes present to us in the here and now. We also widen our capacity to experience God's love and caring in the present.

Remembering relaxes us. The famous Brazilian soccer player, Pele, often prepares for games by remembering, remembering times from his childhood when he played soccer barefoot along Brazilian beaches, or some of his best experiences of winning. For especially difficult games he would take up to thirty minutes of remembering.

The Scriptures frequently speak of remembering. The Psalmists remember the goodness of God; they remember his mercy. So much of the prayer of the Psalmists was simply remembering. The Hebrew word for remembering is **zicar**; it means remembering in such a strong way as the past becomes present.

Says the Psalmist: "I remember the days gone by; I think about all that you have done, I bring to mind your deeds...remind me...of your constant love, for I put my trust in you." (Psalm 143; 5-8)

Prayer Experience

Find a comfortable place. Relax. Take some time for the ease of centering prayer. Gently let your mind float back to times you especially felt God's loving presence. Perhaps it was a walk at night when all the stars were out...your first communion...a prayer time...a retreat...a time when you felt God's love coming to you through another person...a time of crisis in which you felt an unexpected comfort...perhaps listening to a special song or music...Remember the sights, the taste, the sounds, the feelings. Feel the feelings again. Relieve the experience. This is a way of praying, a prayer script you can return to many times and call forth many strengthening memories from the past to help you live more fully in the present and the future.

CHAPTER TEN

The Healing Therapy of God's Forgiveness

So many of the people God uses as special instruments of His Presence constantly speak of how much they have been forgiven. They remember and cherish God's forgiveness. Like Mary Magdalene, "Those who have been forgiven much love much."

St. Francis of Assisi experienced the healing therapy of forgiveness and awoke to a world fresh with wonder. This playboy turned into a joyful troubador of God's love. He and the community around him changed their world.

In his prayer and in his conversation Francis frequently recalled how God's mercy overwhelmed him and redirected him.

One day as Francis and his big burly companion Masseo walked barefooted on a dusty Italian road, Masseo turned to him and said, "Francis, why you? Why is the whole world following after you? Let's face it, Francis, you're not a very handsome person. You're not much to look at. You're not very educated; you don't even know much Latin. Why you, Francis? Why is the whole world following after you?"

Francis paused a moment, turned his eyes to Masseo and said, "It's like this, Masseo, the Most High looked down from heaven and he couldn't find anyone more foolish or full of folly, more inadequate, and he had mercy on me; and expressed His love to me. That's so it could clearly be seen, Masseo, that what good I do is of the Most High and not of me."

An attitude like Francis, is an attitude that can make us mirrors that reflect God's love. It's the realization that we are what we are because of God's constant forgiveness. It's through such brokenness, through such earthen vessesls, God's love flows.

There is a wall plaque I see in many homes that reads, "Chrisitians are not perfect, they're just forgiven." Even though it has become a cliche', the phrase on that plaque is profoundly true. The reality of sin is ever before each of us. Sin comes from putting ourselves first. When I center on myself to the exclusion of God and others I build barriers between myself and God -- between myself and those around me. If I hurt and use others, I hurt and use God. Selfish centering on myself is sin. It is deadening and brings death.

And by ourselves we cannot patch up the wounds that sin brings. There is but one remedy for sin, God's overwhelming forgiveness. He waits to greet us like the father waiting to greet the prodigal son. He wants to take us in His arms and cradle us like the shepherd that cradles the lost sheep. He wants us to leap into His forgiving, loving arms.

Our problem is that we are afraid to look at our sinfulness. We don't fully understand how intensly God is ready to forgive us. God is eager to forgive us. "There is more joy in heaven over one sinner who repents than over ninety-nine just who have no need of repentance." (Matthew 18:13).

Another part of the mystery of forgiveness is that if we acknowledge our sin and receive God's forgiveness, a deeper love, a deeper compassion grows in our hearts. Just as Jesus said of Mary Magdalene, "Her sins which are many or forgiven, for she has loved much, but those who are forgiven little, love little."

In asking forgiveness we become vulnerable, woundable. We have to acknowledge that we don't have it all under control; we have to acknowledge the depth of our need. When we do this, when we receive the tender forgiveness of the father, this deepens and escalates our capacity to love. As Paul the Apostle said, "Where sin did abound, grace did that much more abound."

The following is a prayer script that will help you remember the ways God has forgiven you. A sense of being forgiven leaves us feeling bright, clean, and refreshed.

Remembering those times of forgiveness strengthens our

thankfulness; and makes it easier for us to turn to Him when our selfishness again puts up barriers. Remembering God's mercy can be a constant source for a deepening and ever-increasing compassion, a source of a deep at-homeness with yourself, a source of a great ability to accept and forgive others.

Prayer Experience
PART I

Relax... Rest in God's love... When you are relaxed, resting in the love of God, let your mind remember times that you have experienced forgiveness. Perhaps during and after the Sacrament of Reconciliation. Perhaps when you have felt the unexpected forgiveness of a family member or friend after you hurt them. Perhaps a time when you overcame a serious problem through God's forgiveness. Let your mind float back to the peace of those times. Center on the sense of at-homeness and peace.

PART II

After you have experienced the joyful memories of the grace of forgiveness in times past; you are ready to experience forgiveness in the now.

Relax... Repeat a short prayer phrase for a few moments... Become aware of your body... your emotions... your thoughts... Pause and ask God to bring to awareness one or more ways you have been putting yourself first in ways that harm others, God or yourself... In your own words ask His forgiveness... Sense the loving peace of His healing light surround you. Bathe in that healing light as long as you wish.

If you belong to sacramental church; celebrate and seal God's forgiveness in the Sacrament of Reconciliation.

SECTION III

GOD'S LOVE OPENS
NEW DIMENSIONS

CHAPER ELEVEN

A Love That Gives Birth To Wonder

God's love transcends our logical knowledge. When we open ourselves up to Him, we open ourselves up to the dimension of the wondrous, to the spiritual world, to an experience above words. When I think of wonder, I think of children two to five years old. The sense of life's mystery has not been bleached out of them. They take a leaf, hold it in their hands, delighting in it; they grab a spring flower and giggle with joy. Just watching a train pass by becomes an adventure. Society educates much of the sense of wonder out of us.

When we open ourselves to God's love, to prayer, wonder is born again in us.

In his moving novel, **Creek Mary's Blood**, Dee Brown tells the story of a Cherokee Indian who entered into the wonder of the spiritual world. The book is the **Gone with the Wind** of the American Indians. Part of the story involves a well-educated Cherokee named Dane who acted as a scout for some of the wagon trains moving out West. Later he married a Cheyenne and joined the Cheyenne tribe.

The Cheyenne religion, like much North American Indian spirituality, resembles Christian spirituality.

An important event in the life of Dane took place when he entered into what he called "the real world". By this he meant the spiritual world — the dimension of the wondrous:

Dane tells a reporter about his spiritual discovery:

"I lived with the Cheyenne a long time before I learned how
to cross into the real world, and all that time my wife and

children could do this and they were puzzled because I could not join them there...I was finally able to find my way into the real world with my family. I discovered mysterious powers within my memory and learned that when you pray for others to become strong you become strong, too, because that connects you with everything else. You become a part of everything and that is how I knew that I was necessary to my family and they were necessary to me...

"What is it like, the real world?" the reporter asked.

He remained silent for a while and then spoke slowly.

"Being a man who loves words, I have often thought about that. But some things cannot be put into words. The closet I ever came was an English word. Shimmering."

"Shimmering?"

"Yes, like swimming in moonlight."

(**Creek Mary's Blood** Dee Brown, Holt Rinehart and Winston)

The following series of meditations will help you to experience dimensions of God's love that are beyond the singing of it. These meditations send the message to your deep self that there is always more, always a beyond, that reality is ever new.

CHAPTER TWELVE

Nature - A Pathway For God's Love

Scenes from nature, sounds from nature, are bright threads woven throughout the cloth of Scripture. It seems as though the Scriptures cannot speak of God without using images and comparisons from nature, such as, "I will lift up my eyes to the hills, from whence comes my help. My help comes from the Lord," or "As the mountains are round about Jerusalem, so is the Lord around about His people."

Psalm 104 exclaims: "Praise the Lord, my soul! Oh, Lord my God, how great you are! You are clothed with majesty and glory; you cover yourself with light; you use the clouds as your chariot and ride on the wings of the wind; you use the wind as your messengers and flashes of lightening as your servants. You make springs flow in the valleys, and rivers run between the hills... from the sky you send rain on the hills, and the earth is filled with your blessings..."

As the sensitive, God-filled poet Gerard Manly Hopkins tells us: "The world is charged with grandeur of God. It will flame out, like shining from shook foil; it gathers to a greatness, like the ooze of oil... Because the Holy Ghost over the bent world broods with warm breast and with ah! bright wings."

As Bonaventure wrote: "In creation we see the footprints of God." Nature can be a source, channel for God's presence coming to us. Remembering nature expands our capacity of God, expands our capacity for experiencing Him every day in His creation.

Prayer Script

When you are relaxed, prayerful and in the loving presence of God, begin to imagine some of the beautiful scenes of nature you have seen; the sunrises... the sunsets... the hot beating sun coming down on you in summertime... the sound and sight of waves beating against the sand... the sky at night... the smell of raindrops on a dusty sidewalk... the fresh air of high mountains... the beauty of mountains against the sky... special times in nature. Relive such times in your imagination -- taste, sights, scents, sounds. Relive the emotions; feel them again.

Remember a nature spot that is special to you. Go there in your imagination. Relax there for awhile and allow that scene to express God's love to you.

CHAPTER THIRTEEN

The Kindly Light That Heals

Light imagery permeates Christian writing and prayer. References to light fill the Scriptures, particularly the Psalms. Psalm 119 says: "Your word is a lamp to guide me, a light in my path."

The shekinah presence of the Lord in the form of light guarded the children of Israel in their exodus, their liberation journey from Egypt. In the New Testament, light surrounded Jesus on Mt. Tabor. Light poured down on Paul when he fell off the horse during his conversion. Second Corinthians says that we behold the splendor of God shining on the face of Jesus.

Throughout the Christian centuries light metaphors and the actual experience of "inner light" are a basic part of Chrisitan spiritual teaching.

Henry Vaughn, the Anglican poet, author of the loveliest of the 17th century devotional poems, constantly speaks of experiencing God through light. His well known poem "The World" says:

"I saw Eternity the other night like a great ring of pure and endless light. All calm as it was bright."

Jacob Beohme, German Protestant spiritual writer of the 17th century spoke of "inward light", "God's Light in the Soul" and "the Light of the Majesty."

Evelyn Underhill in her classic book **Mysticism** documents light in the prayer experiences of the great Christian saints and herself calls this inward light "that light whose smile kindles the Universe".

Light - A Way of Praying

Light was more than a metaphor: Light was a way of praying. Jacob Boehme prayed by focusing on a spot of light reflected from a crystal drinking glass. Architects designed Gothic cathedras so that multi-colored light flooded the faithful. Eastern Orthodox churches evoke the sense of the wonder of Divine light by scores of candles reflecting off shiny gold and silver coins.

St. Seraphim of Sarov, the gentle "nature saint" of Russia, often called the Russian St. Francis suggests imagining light as a way of praying. He says:

". . .a man should shut his eyes and concentrate on bringing his mind down into the depths of his heart, ardently calling on the name of our Lord Jesus Christ...When the mind is concentrated in the heart through this exercise, then the light of Christ begins to shine, lighting up the temple of the soul with its divine radiance... When a man contemplates this eternal light within him his mind remains pure..." **(The Life of St. Seraphim** St. Vladimir's Press)

Many of the meditations throughout this book use light imagery. It is a basic building block in imagination prayer. This following prayer experience is one you will want to use often.

Prayer Experience
PART I

Take time to relax and be still... Repeat a short prayer phrase... Picture yourself surrounded by God's presence in the form of light, an egg-shaped oval of light encircles you... If your imagination is fuzzy today, just have the sense that you are surrounded by invisible light. You don't have to picture the light with real precision to enter into the mystery of it. just a sense of being surrounded by light is enough...

The warm light of His love absorbs your fears, anger and negativity like a sponge... The light richly relaxes and refreshes you... You tingle with newness... The light tells you in a beautiful, eternal way, a way beyond words, of God's immense unfathomable tender and special love for you... Rest for a long time, sensing yourself bathed in His light...

PART II

When you have become comfortable using the first meditation, you can follow it with this second meditation. Go throught the first meditation, relax, picture yourself surrounded by an oval light... Relax in that light... After you are comfortable in this light, begin to be aware of your breathing, your breathing in and your breathing out. The word for the Holy Spirit in the Scriptures is the same word for breathe. Allow your breathing in and out to remind you of the Holy Spirit. Just notice your breathing... Now have a sense every time you breathe in that you are breathing in the light that surrounds you. As you breathe it in, a warm, glowing center grows in the deep middle of your chest, warming your heart... The more you breathe in the light, the more the glowing place in the center of your chest glows, relaxing you, healing you, warming your being with God's love... Every time you exhale, have a sense that you are breathing out negativity and fear. Every time you breathe in you are breathing in light; every time you breathe out you are breating out negativity and fear...

Take as long as you like breathing in the love of God...

PART III

You may want to go even further with this light meditation. So many of our emotions, positive and negative, are located in the muscles of our bodies. Now take this light and in your imagination breathe the light down to your feet. Feel your whole feet area filled with the love of God... Breathe the light down to your calves... Fill them up with the love of God... Breathe the light down to your thighs. Fill them up with the love of God... Breathe the light down to your genitals. Fill them with the love of God...

CHAPTER FOURTEEN

Experiencing the Vastness of God's Love

A powerful image in the Christian tradition for experiencing the vastness of God's love has been the imagery of the ocean, the sea. As John Wesly put it, "We lose ourselves in the ocean of divinity." Or as the contemporary hymn says, "There is a wideness in God's mercy like the wideness of the sea."

Prayer Experience

Take a few minutes to relax... Imagine that you are in a wondrous place, a special place. You are on a huge, beautiful beach made of white powdery sand. There is a vast ocean stretched out before you. You are lying stretched out on the beach with your feet in the water -- hear the sound of the crashing white-caps... the smell of the salt air fills your nostrils... hear the squawking of gulls as they glide high above the sea. The water is warm. The waves begin to break over you. You realize that this is a special ocean, this is the ocean of God's love. It is endless. Feel the waves breaking over your whole body, one after the other. The water is warm and healing. It is as though the waves flow not only on your outside but on your inside too. They go right through you... their gentle motion carries away anxiety, tension. Each wave fills you with joy. Those waves tell you of His love without words. They leave you deeply peaceful... Rest for as long as you wish on the beach, allowing the waves of God's love to sweep over you and heal you.

CHAPTER FIFTEEN

Jesus Shows You The Way To The Father

In this meditation you imagine Jesus. Imagining Jesus is a very traditional way of approaching God. The following meditation knits together many of the images we have already used into a synthesis, a whole.

Prayer Experience
(PART I)

Relax ... Enter deeply into the restfulness of God's love.

Gently, now, I would like for you to picture yourself in a beautiful meadow, the meadow of the 23rd Psalm. It's springtime. The grass is green. The sky is clear and blue. Beautiful trees surround you. There is a stream gurgling into a quiet pond. You lie out in the grass taking a sunbath. It is a special place, God's place. The warm sunlight beams down on you. It is the sunlight of God's own love. Just lie there, taking a sunbath in God's love ... Allow His healing sunlight to heal you. Remain in the sunlight of His as long as you wish ...

This light leaves you feeling fresh, clean; you have never felt so good, so much in awe of God's creation, so much in wonder at God Himself. You marvel at the beauty of God's creation all around you. The trees ... The birds ... The stream ... Hear the rustle of the grass.

(PART II)

Someone is moving toward you in his bare feet. A sense of fear and awe come over you. You stand up and look and there is Jesus ... Picture Him any way you would like to ...

At first when you look at Him you have a sense of your unworthiness, of the bad things you've done in your life ... But you look into His eyes. And His eyes are full of untellable love. His eyes say, "I love you, I care for you. It's all right. I'm burning with love for you from all eternity." His eyes bring deep forgiveness and peace and unspeakable joy to you. He embraces you. Feel His arms tenderly and tightly around you. Rest in His embrace for as long as you wish ...

(PART III)

He passes from being in your arms to being in your heart, from a physical presence to a spiritual one. Feel Him in your heart ...

He speaks to you from the depth of your heart. "I will show you the love of the Father." After He has said this, you feel yourself getting lighter and lighter and lighter. You are so light you begin to float. All your cares leave you as you are floating, floating with the ease of a hot air balloon. You go higher and higher and higher, floating gently, smoothly. You go through a few white clouds, float gently with them. You go higher and higher and higher ... The higher you go the more at ease you feel ... You come to a place that is filled with an endless sea of bright white light. You float into the center of this sea of light. It is all around you. The light penetrates you. The light speaks to you of a love far beyond the telling of it. The light expresses to you the love of the Father. Float in the light. Let the light permeate you. As you float in it, as you bathe in it, let the light speak to your heart of the love of the Father. Remain in this light, the light of the Father's love, as long as you wish ...

SECTION IV

PEOPLE AND PRAYER

CHAPTER SIXTEEN

Relationships And Prayer

Augustine once wrote, "The love with which we love God and love one another is the same love." Mature spirituality involves experiencing God in human relationships, as well as in solitude. Prayer that moves us away from people can become escapism. Prayer and people belong together. Relationship is not a means to a goal, it is the goal.

Leslie Weatherhead, the well-known Methodist minister, told this story about the trenches in World War I France.

Two friends in the American army were caught in the muddy hell of trench warfare. They were commanded to charge over the barbed wire; the resistance was ferocious, and they retreated. One of the two friends was seriously wounded and left behind. The other friend, disobeying a direct order from the officer, went after him to drag him over the barbed wire back to the trench. When he came back to the trench with his friend on his shoulder, his friend was dead, and he himself had been mortally wounded while dragging him back.

The officer said, "It wasn't worth it, was it?" The soldier looked him in the eye and said, "Yes, it was worth it, because when I got there he said, 'Jim, I knew you would come.'"

We relate to one another not to win a war, not to implement a program or finish a project, but because it's our eternal calling. Relationship is its own end.

Treasure in Clay Pots

In the midst of the earthy coarseness of daily life, in the midst of their humanity, people can become channels of God's love. Perhaps they don't consciously know it. Perhaps they are not even outwardly religious people, but they have been to us a sign of His love and a means of His love. They incarnate, enflesh, and make God's caring touchable. Many little saviours have incarnated the love of the One Saviour. Paul the Apostle, in beginning and closing his letters, often said, "I think of you whenever I pray to God." He could also say, "You are to me the aroma of Christ." That great saint who lived in the fourth century, St. Paulinas of Nola, in a beautiful letter to a friend said, "In your personality, Christ comes to me. I meet Him in your person."

We encounter God in prayer and we can encounter people in prayer. We should not run from the people who make up the fabric of daily living when we pray, but take them into our prayer. They are fuel for meditation. They are grist for the mill. Prayer thrives on the horizontal dimension. Just like Paul, we can remember people in our prayer, the times of closeness and strength. Remembering brings those healing times into the present. In our prayer we can experience again the people who have been to us channels of God's love. We can practice loving people in our prayer. We can bring hurt relationships to a loving God for mending.

Imagination and Relationships

It is so easy for us to live on a physical and intellectual level in our relationships. And often we miss the intuitive subconscious cues that come to us. Imagination helps us transcend these problems and transcend our separateness.

My friend, Bill, uses his imagination to heal relationships. In one instance, his relationship with his boss, a man 15 years older than he, was strained. A close friendship was deteriorating. His boss constantly belittled him, and Bill reacted defensively. Cold anger took him over. Spontaneity was drained from their friendship.

Bill took an hour one afternoon to relax and pray, and in his imagination he went into the boss' office and looked him in the eye and said, "John, what's the problem?" In his imagination his boss broke down and cried and said, "I'm not going to go any further in this company. My life seems over. My youth and vitality and all the potential which I have are wasted. I'm lonely." These words broke Bill's heart open. He realized that his boss felt like a failure and was crying out for affirmation and compassion.

The next day Bill was met with many of the same belittling comments, but he could look past those to the hurt that caused those comments. He began to feel heartfelt compassion and sensitivity for his boss. His prayer session had helped him become aware of subconscious intuitive signals. He got to the heart of the problem and now reacted with affirmation. His attitude began to change his boss.

The boss slowly stopped his belittling comments. The two began to have many heart-to-heart talks. The relationship blossomed and became even more spontaneous and alive than before.

CHAPTER SEVENTEEN

Taking People Into Your Prayer

During my three years in Junior High, I treaded rough waters. My stomach stayed twisted with the ache of fear and hopelessness.

I watched my Cherokee grandfather, who was a second father to me, die a painful death of cancer. My mother was seriously ill with ulcers and, her weight dropped fifty pounds from 140 to 90. For two years it seemed that we would soon be losing her too. She later experienced a full recovery.

My grades plummeted. I went from A's to D's. Fear soaked away my energy to relate to people my age. I lost my friends. My classmates noticed my worried preoccupation but were too young to understand.

Those years before high school were years of sinking into an endless black hole. I was fourteen, and it seemed that my life was over. An emotionally caused speech impediment kept me from being able to carry on many ordinary conversations.

Then I moved on to High School and met Margaret Cox, my feisty and sand-voiced creative writing teacher. It is hard to believe that over twenty years have passed since I met her during my first year of high school. She saw past the panic that immobilized me and recognized the beauty that was in me. Her belief in me was the magnet that drew out the real me. She helped me develop my writing talents, forced me against my will to enter speaking contests, and treated me as a friend as well as a student. Basking in her loving gaze, I blossomed.

By the time I had graduated from high school, my world had changed. My grades jumped from D's to A's. I won writing contests, my speech impediment went away, and I won a statewide oratorical contest. The grave clothes that had surrounded me as they had surrounded Lazarus had been unwrapped by her caring.

Now that I am grown, when I am discouraged and overcome with fear of failure, I remember her. The solid tenderness in her eyes, the strength in her voice, and the healing flows to me again.

Each of us have many people in our past who have been sources of healing for us. Remembering brings that healing to you again. Taking time to recall these moments enlarges our capacity for loving here and now.

Prayer Experience

Relax, be still ... go back to your childhood. Let there emerge into your consciousness scenes where you felt loved by another person. Who was it? Remember how they looked, their face, their body. Recall the scenes, the sights, along with the smells. Relive.

There are also people in the here and now who are channels of grace for you. Imagine someone in your life right now you are close to. In your imagination, go to them at work, at home, at the rectory, the convent. Go wherever you think they are. Look them in the eye in your imagination. Experience the strength and warmth of their eyes. Embrace them and feel their arms touch you. Say the loving and affirming things you would like to say in real life, but don't always think of.

CHAPTER EIGHTEEN

Prayer That Helps With Everyday Loving

Not only are other people channels for God's love to us, but we can be channels of God's love to others. The fruit of prayer is not beautiful religious experiences while we pray, though if those should happen they should be received with gratitude. But the true fruit of prayer comes in everydayness.

Prayer Experience
Think ahead about tomorrow. Go over your day, getting up in the morning, work, school, whatever ... Let some scenes and some of the people that might be in those scenes flash through your mind.

Now replay some of those scenes you've just imagined. This time you're going to love the people you meet in the scenes the way you would like to love them. See yourself as a channel of God's presence, a manifestation of His love, His hands, His feet. Love as you would like to love. Care as you would like to care.

Perhaps you're a person that's shy and never talks much. In your imagination, go a little bit more outside of yourself to love people ... Perhaps you talk too much and dominate conversations. Picture yourself being a better listener ...

Picture other ways of loving ... And week by week you'll find yourself a more caring person. But don't be disappointed if you don't love as well in reality as you do in your imagination. Remember we are those clay pots that Paul spoke about, the treasure we possess is in those clay pots.

In going through this prayer experience you have doubtlessly become aware of ways that you fail in loving. One of the reasons that we feel pain, tension and guilt in our relationships is that we expect far too much of ourselves, far more than God does. His call to us is to relax and allow His transforming love to make us channels of His love. How well He understands that our capacity to love others is imperfect. How much He forgives us when we fail by not loving others as we should. Pause a moment and allow God's forgiveness to flow over hurt places inside you, the places in which you feel failure for not loving as you would like.

CHAPTER NINETEEN

The Power Of Affirmation

How many times have you heard the phrase, "to love others you must learn to love yourself?" Most of us have heard this so many times that it has become cliche'. Many of us have found that loving ourselves is not an easy matter!

A key part of loving ourselves is seeing the goodness within ourselves, learning to affirm ourselves. So many times we are overcome with self-criticism, self-doubt, and fear. At times these emotions paralyze us. Learning to affirm ourselves is a key to our establishing strong loving relationships with others.

Our self-image, that is, how we see ourselves, how we feel about ourselves, is often complex and multi-faceted. Affirmations, and creative visualization are a wonderful way of creating a more positive and loving self image.

The following prayer experience is one to help you grow in the art of loving yourself. It is often easier to appreciate the good qualities in others and see their faults and shortcomings in perspective. We are usually harder with ourselves.

Loving yourself can work wonders in your life.

Prayer Experience

Take time to relax, be still. Then review your day so far. Or if it's the morning, review yesterday. Think about how you felt and about yourself at different times during the day. Just notice what ideas and images you held about yourself at different times.

See if you notice overly critical, harsh, judgments about yourself. Notice their power to ensnare you and to harm you. Picture a helium balloon whose gondola is a big trash can. And in your imagination take these harsh judgments of yourself as though you were pulling them from your stomach or chest area and deposit them in the trash can, one by one...

Now take a knife and cut the ropes that are holding down the trash can and the balloon and see those harsh self judgments float away. Feel yourself feeling light and joyous as they float away.

Imagine that you are in an everyday situation. Someone comes up to you with a look of love and affirmation in their eyes to tell you something very good about you. More people join in. They tell you how much they like you and what a good person you are. Soak in what they say. More and more people come and look on you with love a respect in their eyes. What sort of good things do they say about you? Rest now. Rest a moment in the sense of your own worth that you feel, realizing deeply that God made you and God made you good.

CHAPTER TWENTY

Affirming Others

Mark Twain once said, "I can live two months on one compliment." Mahatma Gandhi, who inspired millions of people to go beyond themselves and accomplish unheard of feats, mastered the art of affirmation. Louis Fisher, one of Gandhi's biographers, gives a clue to his ability to transform people. He says, "He refused to see the bad in people. He often changed human beings by regarding them not as what they were but as though they were what they wished to be, and as though the good in them was all of them."

Perhaps the greatest key in enjoying friendship and love from others is warmly and honestly telling them about the beauty we see in them. Honestly and openly expressing genuine emotions of warmth we feel toward others is a key that can open up many new doors for friendship and relationship.

Prayer Experience

Relax ... Allow different people in your life to emerge into your imagination, one at a time. Look into their eyes. Be aware of the goodness you see in them and tell them. What change does your telling them make in the look on their face? Be aware of how it affects their relating to you. Notice the effect of this open, beautiful honesty on your own heart. Be still and rest in this good feeling.

CHAPTER TWENTY-ONE

Healing Relationships

Long ago a farmer transported his produce to market in one long haul. His steady horse faithfully pulled the loaded wagon. Each year he added more produce to the wagon as his farm prospered.

Then one year his horse keeled over on the way to the market. The burden laid on the horse had grown so large he dropped dead.

So many human relationships are like this. We pile load after load on the people we love till the relationship dies. Perhaps a marriage ends or grows icy cold. Or a friendship dies and we hide our eyes when we run into our friend at the grocery store or shopping mall. We despair of being close to others again.

In relationships we can pile emotional load after emotional load on one another. One way we burden one another is by possessiveness. Each of us has a Grand Canyon of need for love within us. Only God, ultimately, can fill that need. We easily cling and clutch to others in an attempt to mee that need. Neither husband, wife, friend or relative can fill that need — only God can fill it.

Possessiveness does not allow the other person to be free. We love them not for themselves but because they fill a need.

A classic example of possessiveness is found in Henrik Ibsen's play "The Doll House". This story is set in nineteenth century Norway. The husband is well-off, accomplished in his profession. He keeps his beautiful wife at home where she keeps house. He pets her, pampers her, gives into her every whim, and wants her to be there to be sure the house is nicely kept while he stays busily preoccupied in his own world.

He is shocked one day when his wife announces she is leaving him. He begs, he cries, he pleads saying "Look what I've done for you!"

She replies, "No, I'm a doll in a doll house. And you have not allowed me to be a real person. I have faults, I have dreams, I have visions, I have interests, I have things I want to accomplish and you have made me into a doll in a doll house and we have raised doll children."

How easily each of us can treat one another like dolls in a doll house. We chisel the other person to the shape of our need and fit them into our world. Genuine Christian love allows others to be themselves, it treasures uniqueness. We are bonded together in love and commitment while remaining ourselves.

We each have tasted the pain of having others chisel away at our uniqueness and we have chiseled at others.

Seeing the World Through Other People's Eyes

A central way of healing relationships, of loving the way God loves, is to see things from other people's point of view. That's what God did in Jesus. He became incarnate, one of us. The Word became a human being. The second chapter of Philippians says that God did not stay in His lofty estate but became what we are, taking on human form in the form of a servant. Hebrews says that Jesus was tempted in all the ways that we are, except without sin.

God is able to love us because He feels what we feel. He sees what we see. He has walked in our moccasins for a while.

To know someone is to love them.

Each of us perceives the world differently. Some of us perceive the world primarily through thinking. Others through intuition. Others through sensation.

Often our failure to understand others is our failure to understand different personality types. And because other people often see reality differently — approach the world differently from us — we build up walls and fail to love them.

The following prayer experience is an incarnation experience, an experience to help you know and love others more deeply.

Prayer Experience

In time you will find this to be an extremely rewarding experience. As with all prayer, this takes practice. Deep in our hearts we know intuitively what makes our friends and loved ones tick. It is simply a matter of allowing ourselves to be in touch with that part of ourself that knows. Relaxing helps profoundly, too.

Choose a person. Remember you can choose a different person each time if you wish. You are going to go through this person's day. Imagine this person when he or she wakes up in the morning, eats breakfast, gets ready for work or school. Get inside this person and feel and sense the world as he or she senses and feels it. Go with this person to the different things he or she might be doing and imagine what this person is feeling. Experience this person's feelings of success or failure. Feel the joys and tensions that this person feels. What are their hopes, their dreams? See this person with their family and friends. Feel what they would be feeling.

CHAPTER TWENTY-TWO

Letting Go Of Hurt

One of the greatest difficulties we have in loving in the present moment is our failure to let go and forgive. Holding onto bitterness poisons our health and impedes us in loving people in the present moment. One of the greatest things that can free you up to receive and give love here and now is forgiving past hurts. The Greek word for forgive is the word that means "Let Go."

Prayer Experience
Relax. Be still ... Allow scenes from your past to emerge, scenes where you were hurt ... Look at the people who hurt you. Look them in the eye and say, "I forgive you, I let go of the hurt." Take them by the hands gently and tenderly and say, "I pray God's blessing upon you."

Each time you use this prayer experience, you can imagine different scenes and different people.

As some of the people pass before your mind's eye you will feel uncomfortable telling them, "I forgive you." The hurts are held so deeply that it is difficult for you to let go of them. Father Anthony DeMelo, in his excellent book, **Sadhana**, *suggests this prayer experience, suggests the following way of letting go of deep hurt and unforgiveness.*

First, imagine that you see Jesus Christ on the cross. Take whatever time you might need to have a sense of Him on the cross.

Now turn to the scene of pain where you are hurt and stay with that scene for a while. Keep alternating between the picture of Jesus on the cross and the scene of your hurt. Soon you will find your resentment slipping away from you, and a feeling of peace and joy will sweep over you. A feeling of lightheartedness will overcome you as the image of Our Lord on the cross enables you to let go of imbedded hurt.

Seeing Others in a New Light

This prayer experience is tied in with the previous prayer experience. After all we not only want to forgive others, we want to see the beauty that God has implanted within them. It is not enough just to forgive. We want to be able to see the person who has harmed us in a new light.

Prayer Experience

Relax. Be still ... Picture in your mind someone who has hurt you. Get as clear a picture as you can. Try to find some little spark of brightness shining through the unpleasant picture of the person you had before ... Then have the light from this spark spread out until it covers the whole person and they look radiant and beautiful ... Hold the image of this person surrounded by light before you for a while ...

Look in their face and see what good qualities you can see there ...

CHAPTER TWENTY-THREE

Resolving Conflict

Take time to relax. Imagine a person with whom you have conflict seated facing you. Imagine light from your heart flowing to their heart and back again. What does this exchange of healing light feel like?

As you are doing this, imagine a blank screen in front of you. See if the problem between you and the other person appears on the screen. What is it? Look at it a moment. Now erase the problem and let the screen be blank again and see if a solution emerges.

Going to the Person in Your Imagination

This scene involves going to the person in your imagination. Go to that person in a place where you think they may work, where they might be at home, at recreation ... Look at their face. Look carefully. See what their eyes and their facial expression tell you ... Now ask them what do you see as the problem in our relationship? What do they say?

Now ask them how can I love you better? ... What do you feel is the solution to the problems between us?

SECTION V

SEXUALITY AND MEDITATION

CHAPTER TWENTY-FOUR

Meditations Can Be Sexual

I wonder how many of you thumbing through this book turned to this chapter first? The subject of sex immensely fascinates us and, if we're honest, also frightens us — all of us are interested in it.

How can sex and prayerful meditation possibly be related to one another, you might logically ask! The answer is simple. Our relationship with God involves everything that is a part of us, and sex is a vital part of us. I am a sexual human being. From the chemicals that flow throughout my body to the sense of love and beauty of life that radiates in my heart, I am a sexual person.

Too often we tend to take a narrow view of sexuality. We think of it only in terms of physical acts. Sexuality involves much more than just intercourse. Every time we experience the warmth of affection — affection toward God, affection toward friends, affection toward wife, toward children, toward creation — we experience our sexuality. Sexuality gives us strength for loving. Sexual meditation opens up this part of ourselves to the healing, transforming love of God as it helps us integrate our sexuality with the whole of our personalities. Through including sexuality in meditation, we learn to express our sexuality in ways that help God's kingdom be born in our midst.

Most of us have at least some fear about our sexuality. In the period just after our infancy we might have been taught that our genitalia are dirty. In later childhood and adolescence, we might be warned, over and over again, of the terrible consequences of our sexuality. We learn to be afraid, ashamed, of that part of ourselves.

Right along with the message that our sexuality is dirty comes a similar message that can equally cripple us. It's the message that television programs, commercial movies, jokes at the office, convey to us — the message that sexuality is a means of using others, a means of dominance, a quick pleasure fix, proof of our liberation, proof of our womanhood or manhood. Something so distant from "the real us", we can engage in sexual activity casually, lightly, without regard for others' feelings, without regard for commitment and caring, without regard of God and God's revelation. Living out this view of sexuality slowly drains us of life and humanity and in the end can leave us as dead as if we were in a coffin.

Both these messages put our sexuality in a separate compartment from the rest of our lives and the rest of our personalities. When we lock our sexuality behind prison walls, we throw the rest of our personalities off balance. When we block off our sexuality, we block off much of our ability to have a loving, heartfelt response to God. We block off much of our ability to lovingly embrace the poor, the lonely, the hurting of the world.

As Donald Goergen in his masterful study of spirituality and sexuality, **The Sexual Celibate**, reminds us: "Gentleness and tenderness are rooted in human sexuality. Compassion is a supreme sign of a well-integrated sexual life" (p. 26).

What is Sexual Meditation?

As we allow the Holy Spirit to purify, heal, and integrate our sexuality, we unlock the prison doors and allow the sensual, loving energy of our sexuality to flow throughout the whole of our personalities.

As Fr. Goergen puts it: "Sexuality and spirituality are not enemies but friends. A development of one does not mean a denial of the other. Both flow from the innermost center of human life. Our goal is not to choose between them but to integrate them, to be both spiritual and sexual, holy and sensual, at one and the same time". **(The Sexual Celibate,** Seabury)

In sexual meditation we choose this path of integration. Many Christian churches today are rediscovering the positive role sexuality has to play in all of our lives. Catechetical material and catechetical guidelines today aren't what they were a generation ago. Twenty, thirty years ago, the teaching most people received on sexuality was a laundry list of don'ts. For instance, among some in the Catholic Church and other churches, the apprehension about sexuality was once so strong that some considered a kiss on the mouth between an engaged couples that lasted over thirty seconds a mortal sin. Some convents even forbid sisters from embracing their relatives or even touching or shaking hands with fellow nuns. Such teaching can make sick people.

Now the guidelines for the Catholic Church and many of the other churches take a very different point of view. We present sexuality as something beautiful, positive, given by God, a reflection of God's own nature; something so good that the genital expression of it should be saved for marriage.

This is a much healthier approach. Instead of constantly haranguing young people with what they're not to do, the churches teach them right expressions of sexuality. They teach them to form warm friendships, to love nature, to experience the goodness of their own bodies. And because of the intensity of intercourse, the genital expression of sexuality is so strong and so powerful, they learn that it requires a commitment that embraces a lifetime — the sacrament of marriage.

Scriptural Roots

This union of sexuality and spirituality is not as modern or radical as it sounds. The Hebrews included their sexuality in their relationship with God. The Book of Hosea, one of the most fascinating in the Bible, also presents this passionate God. In a story that the Book of Hosea recounts, God commands Hosea to take a harlot for a wife. And even though she is unfaithful to him, even though she puts on her paint and sells her wares to every stranger along the road, even though she leaves Hosea, God commands Hosea to go out and reclaim her and love her again, unfaithful though she is.

The writer of the Book of Hosea uses that as an illustration of how God loves His people. He loves them passionately. They are His beloved. He is a spouse to them. And even though they are unfaithful, His is faithful. As Hosea says, "Long have I waited for your coming back to me and living deeply a new life."

Though he refrained from marriage and intercourse the gospels portray Jesus as a well-integrated sexual person — gentle, loving, tender and warm.

As Goergen so touchingly writes:

"He touches people physically, psychologically, and spiritually. He has friends — male and female. One cannot underestimate the importance of John, Lazarus, Martha, and Mary in His life. It is in this sense that His sexuality comes through.

Jesus says explicitly that He wants to be gentle (Mt. 11:28-30) ... He spent much of His time involved with people ... He loved little children coming to Him ...

Monks that are Full Sexual People

Some of the most sexual people I know are Trappist Monks at a monastery in the South. In private conversations they tell of God becoming the lover of their heart. They love God with their work; they love God with the prayers they sing every day; and they love God from the depth of being with their sexuality. Two of them I know consciously allow their sexuality to be a part of their prayer. One of them, a priest that has been there thirty or forty years, takes time in his prayer every day to include his sexuality in his prayer. He asks God to keep his sexual thoughts pure and chaste. He takes time every day to imagine a fountain of living water flowing throughout his body, healing, purifying and channeling his sexuality.

Another Trappist is a hermit in his eighties, living in a little hut about a mile from the monastery proper. One of his favorite positions for prayer is lying out on the grass. Bathing in the sun he experiences the goodness of his whole body, the goodness of his whole being. He feels the totality of his whole person loved by God.

A Word of Caution

Integrating our sexuality is a challenge, a beautiful challenge. Yet, as with every important challenge, there is room for caution.

While we are positive about our sexuality we must also be realistic. Sexuality is a powerful force that can take us over and this must always be kept in mind. Yes it is beautiful and good. Yes it is power for loving and compassion. But even as we awaken, channel, and integrate our sexuality, we must be careful not to use that integration as an excuse for license.

CHAPTER TWENTY-FIVE

The Transformation of Our Sexuality

A major step in our journey into wholeness, our journey deeper into God's love is the transformation or sublimation of our sexual energies.

The people of prayer in the history of the Church speak of God becoming their "Beloved", even their "Lover". They use phrases such as "spiritual marriage" and "spiritual espousal" to describe their sense of oneness with their Creator.

Many like Francis equally know that same "gentle" passion toward people - the poor, the lepers, the wounded of this world. The pictures of St. Francis kissing the sores of a leper and finding in the action a profound sweetness; the image of Mother Teresa of Calcutta tenderly washing the limbs of Calcutta's dying, rapt in loving attention - all show the power of a transformed sexuality.

As the famous psychologist of spirituality, Roberto Assagioli, puts it:

"The love energy derived from sexual sublimation... extends in concentric circles or spheres, encompassing ever larger groups of human beings. In the form of compassion it is poured upon those who suffer ... Finally, it can reach out further until it radiates as brotherly love upon all human beings and upon all living creatures." (Pyschosynthesis, Esalen Books)

All to often when we think of the sublimation or transformation of sexuality we think of someone who chose celibacy or a single person who for some reason has not married.

In reality, many who have had the most profound transformation of their sexuality and are full of tender passionate love of God and people are married and enjoying a full sex life. The experience of the transformation and sublimation of sexuality is open to all — celibate, married and single. Despite the norms of today's culture, sublimation is not a dirty word.

Assagioli compares this transformation of our sexuality to the regulating of the waters of a great river. Regulation prevents flooding and the formation of unhealthy marshes.

A part of the water flows through the hydro-electric dam to its natural destination. The channeling of the flowing water produces electricity that brings light and power to thousands.

So it is with our sexuality. When we leave it untransformed and unchanneled it can lead to floods and unhealthy marshes. Rightly channeled, it can be sublimated into power for lighting and healing the hearts of many.

And still, in the case of married people, a proper amount can flow to its natural destination, maritial intercourse.

Transformed Desire

This channeling and transformation of our sexuality that comes from our closeness to God and people changes our desires.

We see the beauty of God's love in sexually attractive persons. Rather than wanting to consume, possess, or expoit them, they become gentle channels of God's presence. We look upon them with a contemplative gaze.

In a powerful passage, St. John Climacus, an early Father and saint describes this.

"A certain man, seeing a woman of unusual beauty, glorified the Creator for her, the mere sight of her moved him to love God and made him shed a flood of tears. It was indeed astonishing to see how what for another could have been a pitfall to perdition was for him the supernatural cause of crown of glory. If such a man, on similar occasions, feels and acts in the same way, he is risen, and is incorruptible, even before the general resurrection" (St. John Climacus).

Fire - A Symbol of Transformation

Among many spiritual writers in the Christian Tradition, fire is a symbol for the love of God that transforms our sexuality and our emotions. St. John of the Cross sang of "the living flame of love that deeply wounds me in my deepest center."

Fire is often the symbolic description of the transformation of sexual energies into strength for tender love of God and others.

Richard Rolle was a 14th century man of prayer who left volumes on the experience of prayer. He loved people and laughter and devoted his whole life to prayer and hospitality.

One of his prayers beautifully describes this transformation process:

"O everlasting Love, enflame my soul with the love of God, so that nothing save His embraces may set my heart on fire ... Enter my heart and fill it with thy sweetness... Burn up my inward parts and all my heart with the fire that burns forever on Thine altar... come, most sweet and most desired. Come, my Love who art my only comfort ... Enflame with thy fire all my heart; enlighten my innermost parts with Thy radiant light; feed me with Love."

The journey toward greater intimacy with God and greater closeness with people naturally brings about a gentle transformation of our sexuality. Including our sexuality in our meditation can help make us aware of the process and help speed it along.

The following "sexual meditation" is one way of including your sexuality in your prayer. It uses the fire imagery used by Rolle, Wesley, and many others as part of the meditation.

So many of our emotions tend to be centered in different parts of our body. The use of the word heart for emotions of love and our spine, our genitals, the part of our trunk below the rib cage are areas associated with sexual emotions.

This is the area the Old Testament referred to as the loins. It was an area full of important emotions and often associated with the heart.

Many ancient traditions consider this area sacred. Says Ruth Carter Stapleton:

"It is significant that the ancients described the genital area of the human body as the sacral area. The words "sacral" and "sacred" come from the indentical root word meaning "of Divine origin," "devoted to God." Sexual energies, when first blossoming within the body, cause the transformation of a baby - fat boy into a sturdy man, a gawky, angular girl, into a lovely, appealing woman... Ultimately, this basic drive is the power of God. With this understanding we are able not only to live comfortably with our sexuality but to be grateful for it. We can give thanks that we will grow and mature to the place where it will be the power motivating us to highest creativity." (P. 56, **The Experience of Inner Healing**, Word.)

The following meditation uses fire imagery to transform and bring up sexual energy from the "loin" area to the heart. If your imagination is fuzzy, you might look at a candle flame a few minutes before beginning to implant the imagery deep in you.

Prayer Experience — Living Flame of Love
PART I

Sit or lie down comfortably. Relax ... Take some silent time for God to love you.
Imagine a beautiful blue or orange flame (if your imagination is fuzzy today, having a sense of it is enough). This flame begins two or three feet below your spine and encompasses your whole body and comes to a point above your heart. The flame is the loving presence of God's love. It fills your whole body burning away fear, negativity, bitterness - transforming them into love and compassion. Feel the sweetness of the flame... The flame transforms and purifies your sexual energies... Feel the flame moving the sexual energy of your lower trunk to your heart... Your heart burns with a new found love and compassion.

PART II

After completing Part I, imagine yourself loving the people in your life you are called upon to love with a new tenderness... Imagine yourself entering into your creative tasks with a new

strength, a new creativity, a gentle and powerful passion...
In your own words ask God to continue to transform your sex-
uality and integrate it with the whole of your personality.

CHAPTER TWENTY-SIX

Reprogramming Our Sexuality In Light of God's Love

Early childhood and puberty, the times when we discover our bodies and our sexuality, are times of pain for so many of us. Perhaps parents caught us in the act of discovering and experimenting with our bodies, and shamed us. Through one means or another we got the message that sexuality was something evil and dirty rather than a sacred, God-given gift.

In our deep self we carry around with us those distorted memories; and those memories shape our behavior even now, like the huge proverbial boulders under the surface of a river that affect its course and flow. Ruth Carter Stapleton, in her book, **The Experience of Inner Healing**, describes a very devout young Catholic woman, Susan. Susan was afflicted with an enormous amount of guilt about her sexuality in general. She felt that it was something bad and something evil and this played a major role in her problem with complusive masturbation. Of course, the real problem was the enormous guilt she felt over it.

During a conference led by Ruth Carter Stapleton, the young woman went through visualization prayer and returned in her imagination to puberty. She was in her bed, naked, aware of all the changes that were taking place in her body. Jesus and Mary were there in the room with her. They looked on her and saw her as beautiful and good. Mary gave her a kiss on the forehead. She looked up and saw her Lord warmly smiling at her. This and similar meditations helped Susan feel good about her sexuality. Bit by bit the guilt began to drain from her and she began to express her sexuality in higher and more creative ways. Her masturbation problem began to fade as she began to feel better about her sexuality.

This following meditation is designed to implant an image deep within our consciousness of the goodness, the sacredness of our sexuality. In this meditation you go back to puberty and have a beautiful experience of awareness of your sexuality. It's an affirming and beautiful image, one that can help you experience a great sense of wholeness in your life today. It is an image that can help displace painful and shameful images from those turbulent days of growing up. Some researchers feel that a positive imaginative scene vividly imagined, can have as much or more impact than real memory.

Prayer Experience

Find a comfortalbe spot, relax, take a moment for conversational prayer; talk with God about how much you need His love to permeate you and help you feel good about your sexuality. Take some time for centering prayer, repeating a little short prayer over and over again.

It is a beautiful spring day. The sky is an incredible blue. You are walking in the deep woods. Your nose fills with the smell of honeysuckle and wild onions. You joyfully roll down a grassy hill. You are 12 or 13. Who were your friends, who were your teachers?

You walk a while in the woods, coming to a granite quarry. Large rocks surround pools of clear water. You sense that no one is around you within a mile away. You're standing on a high rock above the water. You take off all your clothes. You stand naked on top of the rock. You take a deep breath and dive. Feel the cool air rushing past your skin. Feel the cold clear water surround your body as you plunge into the pool. Your whole body feels tingly and alive. You swim to the edge of the quarry, and lift yourself up on a warm granite rock. You take a sunbath, naked on the warm rocks, the hot sun beams down on you, and reminds you of the love of God. You feel your whole body tingle and radiate with the love of God. You have a wonderful sense of God in you and all around you. Your whole body vibrates with loving energy. It feels good to be naked. It feels holy. You have a sense that this new energy vibrating throughout your body will help you enjoy life and help you love.

You have a sense that a wonderous and beautiful mystery will unfold as your life goes forward. You feel God's presence like you've never felt Him before. It's just like Jesus was standing on a nearby rock looking at you. You feel Him that close. And you feel like He's so pleased with the beautiful changes that will take place in you. You hear a squawk above you and you look up and see a brown wild duck, now a flock of wild ducks, beating their wings and flying above you. On the edge of the pool you hear the rustle of grass as a little squirrel scurries about. What wonderful creatures! You wonder at the vastness of the world. You feel a great sense of awe about nature and creation, an over-powering sensation of oneness with the Creator. You marvel at what a unique, beautiful creation the squirrel and the ducks are, the trees, that surround the quarry. Then you realize what a beautiful creation you are, too. Your faith is renewed. You delight in the spell-binding majesty of God's world. You become aware of His power within you, and you know that this new energy you have felt surging through you today is holy and good. You have a sense of reverence. And the quiet sense that what you have experienced here today is sacred. You decide you always want to use this powerful loving energy you have experienced today in good, creative, and whole ways.

CHAPTER TWENTY-SEVEN

The Marriage Embrace Can Become A Prayer

I sat in the waiting room at the Atlanta airport nervously tapping my fingers on my lap. My chest ached with anxiety. I was about to board an airplane bound for the island nation of Barbados in the South Caribbean. The Bishop of that poor country had invited me and a support team consisting of my co-worker, Robert, and a married couple to lead two weeks of spiritual renewal in their national cathedral.

To say that I felt inadequate would be an understatement. My failings flashed in front of me like slides on a slide projector. "Who am I," I said to my self, "to dare to presume to tell these beautiful and simple people of another culture about loving God? I feel like I'm failing to love God and failing to love those around me here in my own backyard."

I thought of their Bishop's great expense in buying our tickets. I was drowning in self-doubt.

Then I heard familiar footsteps coming down the hall. My body began to feel a soothing calmness. I stood up, turned around and there in front of me stood the couple, Ron and Ann, that was accompanying Robert and me to Barbados. They looked at me with healing gentleness. Intuitively they knew the anxiety that was eating away at me.

As they both embraced me, the negativity drained from me. Ron whispered, "What a beautiful person you are, Eddie. I know you're doubting that right now, but what a gift you are to Ann and me."

As I remained there in their arms for a couple of minutes, a restful sense of my own goodness returned to me. Ron and Ann's love was like a sponge all around me, absorbing my fear and pain.

Ron and Ann are special people in my life. When Ron retired from the Air Force, instead of taking a post-retirement job and making a huge income, he and Ann devoted their life to working with a movement known as Marriage Encounter that helps married couples rediscover the beauty of their marriage.

Ron and Ann's mellow, honest love helps redirect the lives of scores of people — married, single and celibate. They are frank in saying that they feel that much of their ability to affect others with their love comes from their sexual relationship with one another. They allow their lovemaking to become a prayer. And the gentleness of their sexual union is not just for themselves alone. It flows out from them in the form of a deep-rooted compassion, a deep-rooted understanding. Their sexuality gives them the ability to affirm and see the goodness in other people and call other people into that goodness. They take time to pray together daily, time to lovingly share their feelings, to be honest and vulnerable with one another.

The Scriptures of the Christian faith throb with enthusiasm for the sexual genital union of husband and wife. Donald Goegen in the **Sexual Celibate**, beautifully sums up the attitude of one of the first, earliest Old Testament writings on sexuality. This is what he says about that early Biblical attitude: "There should be no shame about it. (That is, sexuality.) It is a gift from God given to man as part of God's creation. Sexuality was given to man in Paradise in order that man should be as God wanted him to be; it is a creation of God ... sexuality is basically good in that it enables man to be more complete, more as God wants him to be, not alone and isolated but in fellowship." (*Donald Goargen*, **The Sexual Celibate**, *Seabury*)

Part of the Scripture that sings out the beauty of the marriage embrace most loudly is the *Song of Songs*. Its poetry is timeless, passionate, sensuous, bursting over with words like these: "How delicious is your love, more delicious than wine! How fragrant your perfumes

... your lips, my promised one, bestir wild honey."

The love that the *Song of Songs* describes is a love that is much more than just physical. It involves relationship. "My beloved is mine, and I am His." (2:16) "I am my beloved's, and my beloved is mine." (6:3).

It is a love that is committed, a love that lasts. "Love as strong as death ... love no flood can quench, nor torrents drown." (8:6-7).

Bringing Prayer into the Bedroom

The point of this chapter is that meditation can greatly enhance sex. Even more, that sex within marriage can become a profound way of meditation, a profound prayer. Even so, it may well shock you to hear that sex and intercourse and prayer belong together. As one otherwise open friend of mine said, when I presented this to him, "Eddie, sex is sex and prayer is prayer and don't mix the two."

David Knight in his excellent book **The Good News About Sex** (St. Anthony's Messenger) rises to a beautiful crescendo in a passage on the prayerfulness of married intercourse. He says: "(a couple) can mediate and express to one another through their physical gestures in sex the love that God Himself has for them both. God makes their expressions of love to one another His own; what they say to each other in sex, God says ... Sexual intercourse for the Christian, is a sacred act from beginning to end ... It is an awesome thing to be able to express to another in this way the depth of the passion and love of God".

It is natural that you may well feel a twinge of amazement to find intercourse and prayer talked about in the same breath. It is naturally understandable. Each one of us, no matter the type of sex life or the quality of our sex life, still has remnants of shame rooted in us about our sexuality. As you experience more and more of God's presence in your times of making love, those twinges of shame will begin to disappear.

One major problem that prevents many couples from having a deeply holy experience when they make love, is that they zero in on goals and payoffs. It's easy to take the attitudes of the marketplace into the bedroom. When this happens, sex becomes merely another challenge to succeed in. Couples aim toward having better and better orgasms. The loving caresses, the loving kisses, that come before orgasm are seen as secondary, a build-up to the big payoff, or as one friend puts it, "the big O." The man feels responsible for bringing the woman to orgasm; the woman feels she's not a real woman unless she has one. And a couple like this may tend to judge the future of their marriage on how well their intercourse succeeds. Instead of attempting to encounter one another in a loving way, sex becomes a difficult challenge, like fighting for a championship.

Another obstacle to meditative sexuality comes when couples hold back their emotions from one another. Having sex with a mountain of unexpressed feelings inside, depersonalizes you, dehumanizes you, and leaves you feeling used by your partner. The attitude you take in prayerful sex is the same attitude you take in your private prayer with God. In prayer you come to God as you are, where you are. You come to Him without pretense; vulnerable and moldable. You surrender to Him in prayer. This lets God do what He wants to do most of all — simply love you. As has been said so many times in this book, you take a sunbath in His love and are healed by His loving gaze.

He surrenders to you; He allows your prayer to touch Him; He makes Himself so that He needs our love in prayer.

God surrendered to us, made Himself touchable by coming as a little baby, winning our trust as only a helpless infant can. He surrendered to us, Himself infinitely woundable, infinitely vulnerable to us by His allowing Himself to be wounded on the cross.

Prayer is mutual surrender between you and God. You surrender your expectations; you surrender your pain; you surrender your fear; you surrender your self-hatred; you surrender your concept of yourself before the One who loves you endlessly.

Prayerful sex comes when couples begin to have the attitude toward one another that they have between themselves and God in Prayer. Prayerful sex is mutual surrender. As Jerry Gillis in **Transcendent Sexuality** (Holt Rinehart and Winston) writes: "The purpose of sex is simply simultaneous surrender. Surrender of your demands, of your rigid role, or your ego. Surrender of memory and anticipation. And with all of this surrendering, you will come to know that you really aren't giving up anything at all, but are gaining a powerful new appreciation for the you that really is."

The Hebrew word for intercourse is *Jadoa*, translated in the King James Bible as "know, knowledge". It means more than just our English word intercourse. It means deep, penetrating knowledge, something far more than a head knowledge, a knowledge that goes straight to the heart.

Prayerful sex is living out the full meaning of this Hebrew Biblical word. It is a loving knowledge of one another, a loving gaze upon one another. It involves the same type of waiting as contemplative, meditative prayer. You taste the specialness of your spouse. And your husband, your wife, becomes transparent — a window through which you can gaze not only upon the beauty of your beloved one next to you, but also the beauty of the great Cosmic Lover, God Himself.

And in such a loving encounter you surrender the masks you have developed to keep yourself from being hurt. You surrender your negative programming and there begins to emerge that unique, loving, uninhibited self, that caring, vulnerable self, that God intended you to be from all creation.

Prayer Experience: Some Practical Ideas for Meditative Loving
PART I

Prayerful sex in marriage is an attitude — not a method or set of actions. An attitude of open loving presence to one another that allows God's love to flow in you and through you.

The following prayer meditations offer ideas that may be helpful in allowing sex to be more prayerful. Some of those ideas may be helpful; others may not. Love-making is deeply personal. It's different for each couple. Out of the suggestions in the following prayer experience use what is helpful and discard what is not.

Not every sexual encounter between husband and wife can be long and flowing. You just don't have time. This is especially true when there are children in the house. Even though everyone doesn't have time for every sexual encounter to be long, flowing, and prayerful, everyone does have time for occasional encounters to be planned so that they are long and uninterrupted. Pick a time when you can be by yourselves for a longer period of time than usual. When you take special longer times for slow loving, that experience spills over into other, more hurried times.

When you come together, begin first by sharing your feelings and your emotions. If you have anger or resentment toward your spouse, get that out. Take time to ask forgiveness and forgive one another for any ways you might have hurt each other. Be sure to share positive, upbuilding thoughts and feelings you've had about one another since you last had a chance to talk. Too often we hide the appreciation we feel toward people even more strongly than we hide our anger. Such sharing of the goodness you see in one another is a way of loving one another into wholeness. It's usually always best to get in touch with the emotions first.

Take time now for silent meditative prayer. It's good to meditate in different parts of the same room. In your time apart, take time to relax; take a sunbath in God's love.

You will be amazed at what a loving awareness you have of the other person in this silent time or preparation. During this time of quiet prayer you might go over some of the other meditations contained in the earlier chapter on sexuality, or any of the meditations in the book or meditations from Scripture. Be open to the Holy Spirit as He leads you. Below are two meditations that you might find especially helpful as you prepare to come together after your quiet time.

Meditations
PART II

Take time to enter into deep relaxation. Remember. Go back over the many times, the many ways that God has touched your life. Remember your times of experiencing this holy, awesome God of love of ours. Smell the smells of those times, taste the tastes. See the sights again. Let your body experience what it was like to encounter God. Get in touch with the rhythms, the vibrations of those deep experiences when you felt cradled by your Father God. Rest in that love again.

Gather up those experiences in your heart and picture yourself tenderly, without words, conveying them to your wife or husband

94.

... Picture yourselves together, tenderly loving one another. Picture yourself caressing and being caressed, kissing and being kissed. In your imagination, let the tenderness of your touch express to your spouse the vibrations, the rhythms of the way that God loves you.

Another prayer experience is to picture your spouse enveloped in the light of God's love. Hold that picture in your mind and gaze upon your spouse surrounded by the healing light of God's love as you would gaze upon a holy picture or upon an icon.

Joining Together
PART III

When you come together after your quiet time apart, share with one another your inspirations, the feelings that you had in that silent time. Now is the time to begin your loving sharing. Be slow, tender, sensitive; take time for gentle touching. With the tenderness of your touch, express the tenderness of God. And when you are caressed and touched, receive that not only as the love of your spouse, receive it with the same reverence as you would the caress of God in the bosom of your soul.

And when you are softly joined, take some time to hold one another without movement, maintaining the same type of waiting loving openness that you maintain toward God in your times of stillness before Him. Let the interchange of love flow richly between you. Many couples say that such times of slowing down and being still while connected opens the way for deep spiritual ecstasy to surge throughout their joined bodies and hearts.

And when you are finished, take time for afterglow. Take time to hold one another, to cuddle. Don't rush off.

To close, go deep into your hearts and picture ways that the reservoir of love built up in you from the union you have shared can give life to others — your children, your parents, friends, and especially those in great need of love — the poor, the lonely, the emotionally handicapped. After looking in your hearts, talk about the ways that you can allow the love you have just celebrated to flow from you to help heal our wounded world. You might close with a prayer of thanks.

You Can't Fail

Remember, just as you cannot fail at prayer, you cannot fail at loving sexual union with your spouse. Forget about the past; your aim should be loving and receiving love. Not every time of sexual sharing is superb. Not every time of sexual sharing is glorious. Just as not every time of prayer is glorious, not every time of prayer is superb.

There are dry deserts in sexual sharing just as there are in prayer and when you don't feel superb feelings or wondrous feelings. When you feel grouchy, when it seems, at least to you, that something may have gone wrong, those times can be tremendous times of union. Let your weakness show; let your need show. If you accept that and accept that as a gift, such times can bring you even more closely together.

SECTION VI

HEALING OURSELVES:
HEALING OUR WORLD

"By the waters of Babylon, there we sat down and wept, when we remembered Zion. On the willows there we hung up our lyres, for there our captors required of us songs, and our tormentors, mirth, saying 'sing us one of the songs of Zion!' 'But how shall we sing the Lord's song in a foreign land.'" Psalm 137.

"The time will come, the ancient teachings say, when the sons and daughters of our oppressors will return to us and say, 'Teach us, so that we might survive; for we have almost ruined the Earth.'" — Black Elk.

CHAPTER TWENTY-EIGHT

The Poor Are Our Healing

The T.V. weather station flashed 11:45 p.m. I blankly watched computerized information about weather and news pass before my eyes, while inside, I felt desolate. The week had been especially draining, and I was bathing in a pond of Saturday night dismal feelings.

The phone rang. Some old friend must be calling to have a long visit on the phone. Good, I needed a pick up. However, I was disappointed. Instead, a weak hesitating voice answered, saying, "Is Robert there? This is Philip." Robert cherished his sleep and didn't want to be awakened for anything less than the Second Coming. "Sorry," I said, "He's fast asleep."

Apologetically he said, "I'll try to catch him later." I sensed the desperation in his wavering voice.

Philip, an old bicycle buddy of Robert's, had been blinded in a car accident six months before. He was calling from the rehabilitation center in Warm Springs, Georgia.

Everything in me wanted to hang up and return to my dismal feelings and the T.V. set but I stayed on the phone. He gave vent to his sorrow. There had been a misunderstanding with his fiancee. He was lonely. I could see the gentleness, the openness in his heart toward God and others, and I affirmed that in him. It must have been a thirty minute phone conversation. We closed and I gently said a prayer for him and led him in a short guided meditation. His weak and wavering voice turned mellow and resonant as he thanked me for listening.

As I sat down in front of the T.V. again I noticed I no longer tasted my despair. I had been carried outside of myself. Remarkably, though it would seem that I was the one that was loving Phil, I think he was the one that was loving me. He was humble enough to let me encounter his poverty, his need. And his need drew me outside of myself, helped me feel wanted, and in making myself present to him I found that God, through him, had brought healing to me.

Ten years ago, if I had attempted to write a book like this on prayer, I would have skipped over chapters on justice and peace. For me justice and peace played little role in the real Christian life. All the emotional fireworks of beginning personal encounter with God numbed me to the cry of the poor for peace and justice and it took the pains and joys of aging and maturing over the years to learn that the poor were a gift, the poor were healing.

Everything is Related

Often when someone first experiences God's love they tend to view the spiritual life as a roadway to personal fulfillment and a happier family life. While prayer does lead to personal fulfillment, true prayer eventually draws us beyond the purely personal. We begin to see that our individual healing is tied in with the healing of the whole world. Only as I open up myself to the cry of the poor, to their pain, can the healing process begin within me.

St. Paulinas of Nola captures our relationship with the poor in a timeless phrase, "association with the needy which heals our wounds." (Paulinas of Nola **Poems**, Paulist, page 195). In short, the poor are our healing!

The poor are our healing because their need for God, their need for grace, their need for love, is up front. How easily we mask our own poverty. Each of us is poor. Each of us is broken. Each of us needs God's love and grace. Each of us needs other people. And how desperately we try to hide these needs from ourselves and from others. Our T.V. sets, our movies, the things that money can buy, can so easily become narcotics that keep us from feeling the very pain and the need that draws us close to God and one another. That's why we fear the poor - because their need is so obvious.

The handicapped, the emotionally wounded, those denied justice, who live in a state of emotional and physical starvation can't hide their need. If we dare make ourselves vulnerable to them, their need tears apart our masks and we experience the depth of our own poverty.

Vulnerability to the poor brings a wondrous grace to us. When our sister's pain and brother's pain becomes our pain we are drawn beyond ourselves.

Experiencing All Creation

We can easily miss our interconnectedness with all creation. The native peoples of North America have richly kept alive the sense of our relationship with all creation. A brilliant Navajo student left the reservation to attend university. But after three years he decided to leave. His friends were upset, saying, "You have thrown away your future. you have so much promise. Why"?

The young Navajo answered their questions by drawing two circles. In one he drew a large person in its center. In the other circle he drew several persons, several animals, trees, a hill. He looked to the circle that had only a man in the center and said, "This is the modern civilized world." And he pointed to the circle that contained people, animals and nature together and said, "This is the Navajo world."

I am of Cherokee descent and an active member in my tribe, the Echota Cherokee. The stories of my people richly season my Christianity.

My Cherokee tradition celebrates the interrelationship of everything in creation. An old Cherokee once told me a creation story that illustrates this. According to him, the Creator's first act in creating the universe was to create a vast spiderweb out of which he made the universe. He knit the whole universe together by a vast spiderweb of light.

The Christian faith richly calls us to the same vision. Ephesians and Colossians in particular show that God's healing, God's redemption involves the whole created universe. We are not saved alone, we are not healed alone. We are healed together in community with other human beings. We are saved and healed together with the whole universe. Pauls says in Ephesians, "God has given us the wisdom to understand fully the mystery, the plan He was pleased to decree in Christ, to be carried out in the families of time: namely, to bring all things in heaven and on earth under Christ's headship" (Ephesians 2:9-10).

And again, "He put all things under Christ's feet and has made Him, thus exalted, head of the church, which is His body: the fullness of Him who fills the universe and all its parts" (Ephesians 2:22-23).

Our earth is a wounded earth. Our addictions have raped our world. Our massive attempts to conquer the earth have scarred creation.

As Paul puts it, "together with all creation, we groan for redemption." Only when we acknowledge that we are part of the net that binds together all of God's creation does real healing flow into our being.

When I am in the woods and then on the mountainside, I often remember how much the Cherokee teach the sacred interrelationship between ourselves and all of creation. In the ancient days before the coming of the settlers, my grandfather used to tell me the Cherokee revered the earth as our mother. She was Mon-o-la, the sacrament of God's presence. If a Cherokee wanted to take an animal for food, he picked one of the smallest, weakest of the herd, so that the others would grow strong. He would have to justify his kill by a prayer to the creator and ask forgiveness of the animal. So sacred was all animal life to him.

Even in intertribal warfare, killing another human being was seen as an act which called for great purification and seeking of forgiveness. In even the fiercest wars only a handful of people were killed. Such was the value of human life.

In his saga of his early boyhood, the Cherokee Indian, Forrest Carter, in the book, **The Education of Little Tree**, tells a story that illustrates the way of the Cherokee. It is a story told him by his grandmother. Her father, named Ground Hog, had a special relationship with the trees. He could hear "tree thought." His trees were beautiful, and they weren't at all selfish. They allowed ground for sumac and persimmon, and hickory and chestnut to feed wild animals. Then one day Ground Hog saw loggers high in the mountains, figuring out their plan to cut down these beautiful white oaks. Ground Hog said that the trees began to cry.

The lumberman built a road to bring their wagons into the mountains. The Cherokees protected the trees. At night time after the loggers left, the Cherokee men, women and children dug trenches across the road. In the daytime the logger would come and fill up their trenches. Then one day a white oak fell across the road, destroying a wagon. After this, the lumbermen stopped trying to build the road and left the white oaks in peace. Then at the next full moon, the Cherokees celebrated. "They danced, and the white oaks sang and touched their branches together, and touched the Cherokee. Grandma said they sang a death chant for the white oak who had given his life for the others." (Forrest Carter, **The Education of Little Tree**, Delacorte)

Meditation for Compassion

I cannot be healed unless I am open to all creation being healed. That opening heals me.

Our society conspires to numb us. We place a high value on optimism, competition and being on top of things. We hear so much bad news on television that we switch off our ability to feel what we hear.

Paul the Apostle called us to weep with those that weep and rejoice with those that rejoice. Unless we are willing to feel the depths of pain, our ability to feel joy and laughter leaves us also. Part of our hesitation is that we see ourselves so breakable. If we took in some of the pain of the world, we fear we would be shattered.

In an excellent book on meditation for social activists, Joanna Macy says, "The pain we feel for our world is living testimony to our interconnectedness with it. If we deny this pain, we become like blocked and atrophied neurons, deprived of life's flow and weakening the larger body in which we belong. If on the other hand, we let it move through us, we affirm our belonging; our collective awareness increases. We can open up to the pain of the world in confidence that it can neither shatter nor isolate us, we are not objects that can break. We are resilient patterns within a master plan." (**Despair and Personal Power in the Nuclear Age,** New Society Press.) When we open ourselves to the pain of the world, we experience resilience, a resilience that comes from Christ's love that upholds and unifies all that is.

The following meditation can help you allow painful information to pass through you without shattering you. A siant once said, "Let all sorrows ripen in me." Prayer can help us make rich compost out of the grief of the world. Prayer, meditation can expand the breadth of our compassion. We accept the pain of the world and allow it to pass through us.

The following meditation for compassion is in part based on a meditation by Joanna Macy.

Meditation for Compassion

Relax. Be still....Imagine that your are surrounded by the light of God's presence. An egg-shaped sphere of the light of His love surrounds you. Have a sense of that love encompassing you...

Now allow images of your fellow human beings who are hur-ing and in need, alienated, sick, imprisoned, on battle fields to emerge.... There is no need to strain for these images. They are there by virtue of the fact we are knitted with creation. Those images are already there, waiting to come forward. Let them gather inside you like a dark liquid. Be open to the pain of the universe, the animals, trees, seas, the air...

Notice your breathing...your breathing in and your breathing out. Every breath in you breathe in God's love. Each breath out you breathe out pain. Then feel the pain leave you as the light of God's love that surrounds you absorbs it, absorbs all the pain inside of you. Your pain, the world's pain that you have taken on... Feel the light of His love that surrounds you, supports you and the whole world... Open yourself up to the realization that in taking on the suffering of the world with Christ you share in His redemption. Don't be afraid of the pain, the heart that breaks can contain the whole world. Your heart is large; trust in it.

CHAPTER TWENTY-NINE

It's O.K. To Feel the Pain

Many people say that we should not concern ourselves with actions and prayer that help heal the world and help bring peace until deep inner healing has taken place in our lives. I understand why people feel that way. Some of the people that take part in the peace movement or the pro-life anti-abortion movement appear to need profound inner healing, seem driven, overcome with anger and bitterness. Sometimes that bitterness is outwardly expressed, sometimes it shows itself more subtly in tone of voice and in tight facial muscles.

Often work and actions for peace become a catharsis, a chance to dump out personal pain, bitterness and anger. The image comes to mind of a crowd of anti-abortion people outside a clinic screaming "Baby Killer" angrily waving signs as though they were weapons. I can understand the bitterness of the protestors. I share their same goal. I want to see all abortions stopped. I want to see life preserved both in the womb and outside of the womb. I want to do whatever I can do to prevent abortion, but at the exact same time, I want us all to help build a world, a caring and loving world where no woman would want to have an abortion.

I know in my own life, I am prone to bitterness. I find that when I feel this bitterness, it is a symptom that I am avoiding entering into greieving for our wounded world. The bitterness protects me from feeling the weight of pain; the pain of children who are starving to death, the pain of the elderly who have no one to speak their names with warmth. The pain of our earth, whose rain forests are being demolished by thousands of acres a day, so cattle can be grazed for the few years before the land turns into desert; just so a group of fast-food restaurants will have inexpensive ground beef. I find that when I do decide to enter into the grief, I feel the pain and let it pass through me. Then I find it is much easier to speak a gentle, honest and strong word that can help transform hearts. A word that rings so true that people hear it at the deepest level of their beings and begin to let themselves feel the grief. As I allow the grief to go deep inside me, it breaks my heart open. As I allow the grief to go deep inside me, I find a hope at the bottom of the well of my heart, a hope that makes no logical sense, a hope that comes from God's everlasting love. Living, vibrant water of hope rushes in at the bottom of the well, a hope that Jesus said would well up into eternal life. Then I find when I speak of peace, when I speak for the rights of both the unborn and the born, I can do so with an ease and compassion that comes from knowing that I don't shoulder the burden alone. I share it together with God and with my brothers and sisters. And when I speak out after going through this process, hearts are changed. A compassion warming my insides, warming my heart, reaches out to those with whom I disagree, it reaches out even to the very people that I feel share a great deal of responsibility for wounding our world.

A friend of mine, a beautiful blond-haired woman in her late fifties, after she had just been to a 3-hour pro-life rally, at which most of the speakers' words were strident, words of accusation, said their words jangled her, made her tense. She said, "Eddie, how much better it would be if they had entered into the pain and were standing there in front of the clinic with tears saying, "Father, forgive them for they know not what they do."

The power for tranforming our world is finally the power of powerlessness. Finally the power of weakness - a power that overcomes the princes of this world, that redeems, that transforms. The powerlessness of Jesus on the cross, the powerlessness of Mary, his mother, waiting at the cross. The waiting mother, the weeping mother. The enormous power of that weakness can transform creation. A friend, a pastor, was planning a sermon based on the scriptures describing Mary standing by the cross. He said, "Eddie, if Mary were here today, walking around here in the United States, what would she say to the industrial leaders, to the politicians? What would she say to the people building bombs that could destroy our earth several times over, to people looking casually and without feeling at the disoriented and homeless people of our streets? I could not picture Mary carrying a sign and waving it angrily. I could not picture Mary like some Viet Nam-era protestors shouting, "baby-killer" at young, frightened soldiers just returning from war. No, the image came in my mind of Mary at the cross weeping and grieving over the injustice done to her son and over injustice that ever has been or ever will be. I saw her outside the missile silos saying nothing, just grieving; the look of compassion on her face, saying far more than a hundred thousand fists raised in a protest rally. I saw her weeping outside an abortion clinic and when she speaks, she speaks little and her words are gentle, strong, honest and few. I believe our hearts will never be whole unless we work for peace and justice. Just as our work for peace will be barren unless we are open to inner healing, the two are bound together forever and always.

Just as our work for peace will be barren unless we are open to inner healing, the two are bound together forever and always.

An old folk story helps illustrate this, a legend of Saint Seraphim. Saint Seraphim was the Saint Francis of Russia. He spent years of prayer in a cabin, a wise man full of love, whose heart was filled with caring, whose very presence ushered in healing. Whose words were like salve to wounded hearts. In the village near his cabin, a woman had lost her little boy, her only child. So devastating was her loss that she shut out the pain and every time we shut out the pain, we become unreal and the world appears unreal to us. Rather than feel the nausea that comes when death has reached close, with its cold, terrifying intimacy, she moved into isolating unreality that shut her out of reach from the people around her. Claiming he was not dead, she went through the village saying, "Surely there is a medicine that can cure him." Instead of burying the boy, she carried him with her, saying to her friends. "You are hiding the medicine from me." Finally a shopkeeper said, "Go see Seraphim, he may have the medicine for you" Her eyes glazed, she went to Seraphim, demanding a medicine for the boy. He said, "Go to the houses in this village and find one house that has not known sorrow, deep tragedy or loss, get a grain of barley from that house, and bring it to me. I will make a medicine of it and he will be healed." She did as he asked and as she went from house to house, asking if there had been no sorrow, and found no house without sorrow. She heard people's stories of the great grief in their own lives. Gradually, she ceased to feel alone in her pain. She began to feel her neighbors' pain. Her pain seemed less immense to her when it was seen as part of the pain that everyone felt, and she finally could begin to grieve. She returned to Seraphim and said, "I have found no one that has not known tragedy." As she said that, she began to weep for the first time over her son. She was no longer isolated by denial. Seraphim held her for a very long time as she sobbed. And after days and weeks of grieving, she began to feel a glimmer of hope, the hope of Resurrection and Easter faith.

Entering into the pain of others helps us feel our own pain. We can feel it and let it flow through us and then move on to a place of hope. This is why for real personal healing, for ongoing inner healing, we are called to feel the pain of the world and take actions, even very small acts to help others. I feel that even at the very beginning of our own healing, we need to reach out to heal our world even if it's the tiniest action.

In our prayer for peace in our work for peace even the feelings of bitterness that emerge can be a source of grace if we own them; if we acknowledge them and take them to God instead of acting on them. Honest acknowledgement hauls us back to a place of grace, a place of helplessness, a place of spiritual neediness. And it's the place of acknowledged neediness, that attracts the tidal wave of God's love. Felt neediness is truly the place of healing.

Another mistake we can make is to be so involved with the world and bringing peace to our outward environment that we take no time for our inner environment. When we blend inner healing with the healing of our world, we are speeded on along the pathway toward wholeness.

Prayer Experience

As you enter the refreshing rest of prayer remember a time when you were carrying a heavy emotional burden, one that weighed you down and the people close to you helped you beat it, lessened your sorrow by their entering into your feelings...

Now remember a time when you had an experience of helping someone bear a burden... How did this help you grow, how did you feel.

Picture Jesus coming to you where you are seated. He takes your hands gently holding them. You feel the press of his skin on your hands... As he holds your hands its O.K. to allow yourself to feel the warm caring love of His heart that comes to you from the touch of His hand.
Now hear him repeat the scripture "Come to me all of you who are tired and heavy-laden and I will give you rest...

Sense the burdens in your life as heavy lead balls feel their weight. Jesus puts a basket in front of you and you pull the heavy balls from your chest till they are all gone. Feel how much lighter you are. Feel the deep prayerful restfulness of this moment. You know that Jesus has taken your burden.

Jesus takes your hand again... Feel the warmth of his hand. And He says to you "Take my yoke upon you and learn of me for my yoke is easy and my burden is light." As he holds your hand He shares with you just some of his concern, his compassion for the world, he shares them with you without words. Rest a moment your hands in His.

CHAPTER THIRTY

Praying and Peacemaking

As the first Christian missionaries began to trickle into the mountian homeland of my ancestors, they brought their Bibles with them. A missionary sat down and read many passages to a Cherokee chief. The old man listened in silence. When the missionary completed the reading, the old chief finally spoke, saying, "Plenty good book. But if the white man has had it so long, why is he so warlike?"

Long before Jesus, the prophets moved beyond the warlike character of early Israel and called for peace. The prophet Hosea, whose book is full of compassion and heartfelt love, minced no words. He says, "Because you have trusted in your chariots and in the multitude of your warriors, therefore, the tumult of war shall rise among your people and all your fortresses shall be destroyed" (Hosea 10:13b to 14a)

Isaiah could say, "Woe to those who go down to Egypt for help and rely on horses, who trust in chariots because they are many and in horsemen because they are very strong, but do not look to the Holy one of Israel or consult in the Lord! (Isaiah 31.1)

The Old Testament is not so much other -- worldly oriented as future oriented. It looks to God's reign not so much as a where but as a when. All history, all the interactions of human beings, moved toward a time when God's reign would make all creation new. Micah gives an earth-shaking description of this coming era," ... they shall beat their swords into plowshares, and their spears into pruning hooks; nation shall not lift up sword against nation, neither shall they learn war any more" (Micah 4:1-3)

This new era broke into the world in Jesus. He brought a way out of the spiral of violence. His teaching pointed to something other than hate producing hate and killing producing killing. He said, "You have heard that it was said, 'an eye for an eye and a tooth for a tooth.' But I say to you, do not resist one who is evil. But if anyone strikes you on the right cheek, turn to him the other also; if one would sue you and take your coat, let him have your cloak as well; and if anyone forces you to go one mile, go with him two miles ... you have heard it said, 'you shall love your neighbor and hat your enemy.' But I say to you, love your enemies and pray for those who persecute you, so that you may be sons of your Father who is in heaven." (Matthew 5:38-45).

And, of course, Jesus said, "Blessed are the peacemakers, for they shall be called children of God."

Jesus did not resist when the soldiers came for Him to arrest Him. Impulsive Peter cut off the ear of the high priest's servant. Jesus responded, "Put your sword back into its place; for all who take up the sword shall perish by the sword." (Matthew 26:52).

Jesus calls us to be peacemakers. Christian prayer can lead us beyond just praying for peace to being instruments of peace.

Peace held the highest importance to the Cherokee. Not only peace among people but peace with the whole created world. Prayer knits us back together with our mother the earth, our father the sky, our grandmother the sun and helps us see clearly again the stars. We see the beauty of whatever is before us.

My full-blood cousin, Dhyani Ywahoo, dedicates her whole life to working for peace. A medicine woman, a woman who has helped to preserve the sacred Cherokee tradition, she and her husband operate a retreat house in Vermont and speak throughout the United States bringing this bright Cherokee tradition of healing peace to bear on the painful brokenness of our world. In a note to me, Dhyani made a striking statement on peace.

Through meditation, chants, dance and prayer, one becomes a sacred spindle, to weave anew the web of beauty and harmony.
A wondrous tapestry of light unfolds and the vision of peace is made real at this time.

We pray not only that God bring peace but that we be spindles that weave peace. Or as St. Francis put it, "Instruments of His peace."

Violence among individuals comes when we project onto others the things we dislike about our own self. We tend to see in others the things within ourselves that we have not yet learned to accept and integrate. Usually the things that infuriate us about others are things that are in us. We try to eradicate these things we do not like within ourselves by eradicating those things in others. At the worst level we not only want to eradicate the behavior in others, but even want to get rid of the problem within ourselves by getting rid of the person we project the problem onto.

And so it is with nations. Prayer helps us deal with our inner defensiveness and violence. In the stillness of prayer, deeper and deeper parts of us taste of God's acceptance. Prayer unhooks us from the fears that lead to warfare in families, warfare among friends, and warfare in our world. Prayer disarms us inside.

When we pray, we are put in touch with hope. We savor God's goodness, God's final triumph over the forces of disruption and alienation in our world.

Prayer Experience

Remember a time when you were in angry warfare with some of the people you love most. Remember back to a time when you were at odds with those close around you and someone helped make peace among you.

What did they do? What did their presence as they were making peace feel like? What went on in you as they made peace? Now picture yourself acting in a way that helps bring peace to people who are at odds with each other. Family, co-workers, friends, people in your parish. Picture yourself making peace. What things do you do? What things to you say? What things do you feel? At what times do you keep silent? Does patience play a role?...

Now picture yourself taking some small action that helps bring the world toward peace. Perhaps helping in a fund drive to help the hungry in underdeveloped coutries... perhaps writing your congressman. There are many directions to take... you may return to this part of the meditation many times before scenes come up that feel jsut right for you. Listening to and responding to our call to become peacemakers takes time...

Now we are moving to an experience of God's presence. God's hope working within us to make peace. Notice your breathing, your breathing in and breathing out. The word for the Holy Spirit in the Scriptures is the word for breath. Notice your breathing in and your breathing out. Let the breathing in and breathing out remind you of the Holy Spirit.

Picture yourself surrounded by a sphere of light. Breathe the light in and out. The whole center of your body glows with that light. Light flows through your entire system, the light of God's presence bringing peace and hope... Have a sense that this light that you continue to breathe in flows out from your heart. Let it surround the building you are in. See the people there surrounded by God's light, surrounded by His preaceful presence. Sense that light coming from him through you to others in bringing peace and healing. Think of members of your family who are hurting each other now. Think of some of your friends who are hurting each other now. Picture that light flowing out of your heart to them, bringing peace. Picture that light surrounding your neighborhood bringing light to those who are tearing one another apart with their words, bringing light to families who not only abuse one another with words but with violence. Picture that light flowing over the whole country, bringing peace... Picture the light surrounding landless peasants, and government soldiers in a Third World country, who are shooting bullets at each other. See that light cause them to drop their weapons and embrace one another...

Picture the light surrounding the missle silos, the light surrounding them causes them to disappear. See the whole world surrouned in the shimmering fullness of the light of God's peace and love. Pause for a moment in awareness of the powerful image you have just prayed. In your own words and in your own way, ask God to help you be an instrument of His peace. Pause a moment and see if there comes from your deepest self, images and pictures, that can lead you into becoming that instrument.

Relax, center, be still... Let your imagination take you back to a time when you experienced a peace, peace within you, peace with those around you, peace with your environment. Rest in that memory. Feel the feelings again, taste the tastes, see the scenes. Rest in that memory a moment.

An Interview
with
Eddie Ensley
by *Steve Tyler*

Steve Tyler is a social worker and freelance journalist. He is married and has two daughters. He has been a long-time friend of Contemplative Brothers.

Q. What is Contemplative Brothers and when did it start?

A. Steve, that's a hard one to answer, do you have 5 hours? Contemplative Brothers started ten years ago here in Columbus, Georgia. Right now, there are two of us. When we speak somewhere, we say we were so excited to be with you, that we brought the whole community. It didn't just start off with two people, as you remember, several other men were with us in a brotherhood but after a while it became very clear that most of them were called to marriage and that Robert and I were called to a life of prayer, ministry and celibacy.

Q. Are you a religious order?

A. No.

Q. Then why do you use the name "Contemplative Brothers"?

A. After a few years, it became plain that Robert and I were called to a celibate lifestyle, a lifestyle of prayer, a lifestyle of community, that in some ways resembled a religious order but was not. We call ourselves Contemplative Brothers, meaning layman who are brothers in the Lord and believe in a life of prayer and who also are celibate.

Q. Eddie, you mentioned a person named Robert. Exactly what role does he play in the present ministry?

A. Robert is now 29 years old and he started at this at 19. I first met Robert when I had returned to Columbus from working at a retreat center in Pennsylvania. I met him at a prayer group we were both visiting in my parish. He was fanning a young woman who was paralyzed from the waist down. The air conditioner was not working that night. I could see the look of concern for her in his eyes. Later, during the prayer time, it became obvious to me that Robert was in a state of advanced deep prayer. From the look in his eyes, from the aura of peace in his face, I knew that this person had a deep calling to prayer, a rare calling, calling rare for anyone and especially someone his age. I suggested that the two of us get together for prayer and sharing. The only place that was available to us was the steps to St. Ann's School and the two of us sat there and just went into a rich silence, a silence that was a thick as molasses, full of God's love, full of God's beauty. And we knew then, without even speaking it, that we were being called out, that we had a service to the ministry to perform.

This was also at a time when I had begun to receive many speaking engagements. I had just published a book, "Sounds of Wonder" and a series of articles in a national Catholic magazines and I was receiving invitations from the people in the church in many locations. A little after the time Robert and I had taken the time to pray together, I had been invited out to put on programs and the archdiocese of Los Angeles. The person who invited me was Father Ralph Tichenor, SJ, a well-known writer on spirituality and Cardinal Manning's Vicar for Spiritual Renewal for the archdiocese. While I was out in California, speaking at many churches, I asked Father Tichenor to listen to a tape of Robert Herrmann describing his prayer life. He played it for other priests and leaders in Southern California and their unanimous consensus was that this was a person with a great amount of intuitive wisdom about prayer, a person who had a prayer life of rare depth. And his response was to invite Robert out that summer to lead a day retreat for the priests, religious sisters and the religious brothers of the Archdiocese of Los Angeles. I was out there at that time too and Robert introduced himself and said, "People, I'm scared. Here I am talking to you priests and my furtherest formal theological education was 8th grade Sunday School." That got quite a laugh, but later, there were tears of wonder and tears of love as they heard the richness of his words on prayer. So Robert, since that time, has spoken at hundreds of locations about prayer. He is the editor of the Contemplative Life newsletter and has hundreds of pages of material on his life in prayer which will be published in about a year. He now also reads and studies serious theological books and articles to bring greater solidity to his teaching.

Q. What is your relationship to the church? Is it an official one or an unofficial one? Exactly what role do you play in the Roman Catholic church and other churches?

A. As a Christian, I believe that all of us have to be related to the larger body of Christ. On our own, we can go off in strange directions unless we have checks and balances of the whole church. I told our bishop of our beginning dream of a community, a brotherhood and he said, "I'm excited about that and please know that I want to serve you and love you in any way". Our relationship with the total church and the person of our bishop has been a warm and good one. All our major decisions are made through a discernment process with our diocese. He appointed a member of his staff, Sister Mercedes, as our liaison with him and we meet with the bishop from time to time. Soon after my talk with the bishop, he asked me to teach aspects of spirituality for the permanent deacon program. We are accountable to the bishop of Savannah for all of our ministry. We have spoken at the last five Spiritual Renewal conferences in our diocese. In addition, we have had discerning spiritual leaders such as Father Richard Rohr, Ralph Tichenor S. J., Duane Stenze O.F.M. spend a week with us to discern our life and give us advice on our ministry.

Q. Eddie, didn't the diocese do something special for you at the last Renewal convention?
A. Yes, they did. It was a surprise and it really warmed my heart. Sister Alice, a beautiful nun in my home parish that I have known for 12 years, gave a short talk about us as a ministry and led a short ceremony of recognition. Everyone gave us a standing ovation. It certainly warmed our hearts and made us feel loved and appreciated. It helped deepen our sense that when we go out and speak in many varied parts of the country that we are supported and loved by the church in South Georgia.

Eddie's Background

Q. What experiences in the past started your spiritual pilgrimage to the present ministry that you are conducting now?
A. As you know, Steve, I studied seven years to be a Presbyterian minister before becoming a Roman Catholic. Most of my family are Southern Baptists. I have several cousins who are Southern Baptist ministers. I never really attended the Baptist Church very much as a child but the broader family was Baptist so some of my roots are Baptist. My Presbyterian and Baptist roots are something I cherish. I don't think that I have left behind any of the things I learned. I think much of the effectiveness our ministry has is in part been because of the deep Protestant roots that I have.

I studied four years undergraduate, majoring in Philosophy, and New Testament scripture studies and after that, three years of post-graduate work in graduate schools of theology and after that, a further years work in history and counseling. counseling.

Q. Eddie, what exactly brought about your change from the Presbyterian faith to the Roman Catholic church?

A. I had had a rich experience as a Presbyterian. I had been given invaluable tools by professors such as Walter Elwell, J. Robert Williams and Ross McKenzie. Primarily, Steve, it was my growing hunger for deep prayer that I had a real sense that my calling was to spend much time in prayer, to really probe the depths of prayer.

I had an experience in Selma, Alabama, stopping into a Roman Catholic church for the first time in my life. It was empty and I just wanted to see what it was like. It looked very much like a Presbyterian church. These were the first days after the Second Vatican council. It even smelled the same, they used the same kind of cleaning fluid I'm sure. And I sat down in a pew and my heart went to a rich and silent place and the very cells of my body felt a real specialness about this church. It felt like no other church I had ever entered before and as my heart rested there for 30 minutes, and afterward, I said to myself, "Eddie, you have to get out of here quickly or you are going to end up to become one of those Roman Catholics."

And as things would have it, just after I was there, when I was back in my college in Jackson, Mississippi, I met a young priest at a Civil Rights march. His name was Bernie Law. And I felt that there was something very profound in his heart, a wholeness and an at-homeness with himself and the world. A holy joy among people who shared his faith, a joy and a deep compassion. These were things I knew not just from what he said but from a look in his eye, the way he walked and seeing him as we prayed. He invited me to supper with him and he was most affirming of my being Presbyterian. Never did he try to make me a Catholic; if anything, he wanted me to bloom where planted. And that's what most all of us should do, bloom where we're planted. But there are exceptions.

Bernie Law became a close friend. He would come up to my dormitory room and get me for coffee. Deep within my heart, I began to sense, especially because of my hunger for prayer, the Catholic Church was my calling and my home. However, I am a stubborn person and it took me about six more years. I was probably the only Presbyterian seminarian that attended daily Mass. And so finally in 1972, when I was visiting Father Bernie from post-graduate school in Texas, I was received into the Roman Catholic Church by Father Law in Jackson, Mississippi.

Q. Eddie, is this the same Bernie Law that is the current Cardinal of Boston?

A. That's right, Steve.

Q. Have you seen Cardinal Law lately?

A. Yes, Steve, I saw him, and I think maybe we should call him Bernard Law,

I saw him just a year ago. I visited him just after he was made Archbishop of Boston. I must say that to be around him is a rich human experience. He is very grounded, very down-to-earth, a very earthy and holy person at the same time. Robert Herrmann was with me and he had us sit down, laid his hands on us and prayed for the special grace of the Holy Spirit. He has encouraged me so much in our ministry through the year and in a very real sense, he is my spiritual father. I am excited that his ministry has so much more scope now that he had been made a Cardinal.

The Importance of Prayer in Eddie's Ministry

Q. Eddie, you've mentioned that this is a ministry of prayer and I wanted to ask you why a ministry of prayer in this day and age when people are too busy to pray. People are too busy to communicate with each other at all, much less to communicate with God?

A. St. John of the Cross said that a person who goes about in an active ministry without prayer, gets hammered down by life and even sometimes does more harm than good. He said that for a person of prayer, one simple action done out of prayer, one simple word, one simple act of love, one simple decision done out of deep prayer equals a thousand actions that are done without prayer. There is a story of the Middle Ages, the story of a great Dominican priest, he was highly educated, he read to all the church fathers. He could recite quotes from Greek philosophy and yet when he spoke, people were not touched, people yawned and nodded in the church. He decided to do something radical. He took a year off and prayed. Then when he went back to the pulpit, tears began to well up in his eyes as he spoke a few words and he looked out and suddenly tears were in everyone's eyes after he spoke those few words. Profound, powerful and deep conversion took place in the people there. His deep heart spoke to their deep heart.

Eddie's Education and Training

Q. What further credentials do you have that qualifies you to give retreats and seminars on spirituality?

A. I guess in short, I could say that the main qualification that I have is one that all of us have, that I am a human being that struggles. But I know that you want me to go into this further. Steve, one of the great things about my theology education as a Presbyterian is that they believe in learning the tools of primary research, of primary source material. For someone to become a Presbyterian minister, they must be fluent in Greek and Hebrew. I was taught by people like Walter Elwell to look at the scriptures in the original language and decide what it meant in light of the writings of that period in the original languages. When I was becoming a Catholic, I had many intellectual questions I had to resolve.

Being a compulsive researcher, I began to go into primary sources, the church fathers, the great people of prayer in the church, holy women like Teresa of Avila, Catherine of Genoa, holy men like St. Francis, reading about them not primarily from modern books about them but reading the early sources. I became interested in how they prayed, how they loved, how they cared for their fellow humans. The theoretical questions were less important to me than the personal ones. I looked at the personal side of church history, reading letters 1500 years old, reading sermons 1200 years old and I found a tremendous amount of wealth we had forgotten. We have an enormous richness of spirituality as Christians, we are spiritual millionaires and we live like spiritual paupers. Our history, our heritage offers us thousands of holy women and holy men, down-to-earth women and down-to-earth men, balanced people that have great treasures to offer us. I became excited about that. I would spend, when I had the chance, 12 hours in old libraries, rare book rooms, at a time.

First Book Published

Q. Eddie, didn't a Catholic publisher discover what you were doing and inform you that he wanted to publish a book about your work?

A. Yes. An editor from Paulist Press, found out about the research I had been doing, called me to New York to talk to them, and before we left they were talking about what color cover to choose for the book. But they were talking about a book that hadn't been written yet. And so I had years of research but I had to put it together. The book was finally published in 1977 and was called, **Sounds of Wonder**.

Q. Eddie, didn't you say that the editor of Paulist Press said that the research that you conducted on the book was the equivalent of two doctoral theses?

A. Yes.

Practical Experience

Q. Eddie, what kind of practical training have you had to conduct retreats? In order to conduct retreats, you need to know more than what is between the covers of books.

A. Part of that, Steve, is experience in field work that I had in college and seminary, I gave many young people's retreats and I had a chance for lots of other types of ministry.

What helped me greatly was when two retreat centers in Pennsylvania asked me to work for them. The first of them was a diocesan house and we gave retreats on the assembly line. It seemed like every day, a school class from their very large Catholic school system would come in to be given a retreat. I had to give a retreat sometimes for weeks, nearly one every day. There were retreats for adults, too.

I also worked for another center in Allentown, a center connected with the Children of Joy community. I had lots of practical experience from two real masters of retreat giving, Tony Cushing and Father Joe Lange.

Q. When did you give your first seminar on contemplative healing?

A. I gave my first seminar on contemplative healing ten years ago in Allentown. 40 people signed up for three months of seminars. There were times tears of love and prayer trickled down from our eyes. Many husbands and wives experienced deep reconciliation with each other. At times, the presence of God was as thick as Southern corn syrup and God was more real than the chairs we were sitting on. We were overwhelmed at how easily people moved into deep praying. Funding for the retreat work that I was doing ceased and at the same time, an article about these seminars was in a national Catholic magazine and invitations suddenly came in from everywhere for me to give retreats.

Different Types of Speaking Engagements

Q. Who usually requests retreats from Contemplative Brothers?

A. There are many different organizations and people. For instance, we were invited by the diocese of Manchester in New Hampshire to speak to all the geographic regions within that diocese. We were there for two weeks. The bishop's vicar for spiritual renewal would take us to different parishes at night-time in different parts of the state and on Sunday afternoons. We ran a one-day retreat so that people could get further exposure. We have done similar ministry in many dioceses. We have worked for the Archdiocese of Los Angeles about five times, and also neighboring dioceses in California.

Sometimes parishes invite us, sometimes renewal committees for certain regions invite us.

We are often invited to speak at large renewal conferences. This is the type of invitation that means the most to us because we get a chance to play a role and working with more people that way. With thousands of people, the power of Christ within all our hearts has brought all of us into rich and resonant timeless moments of healing prayer, when God's love washes over all of us like a cleansing waterfall. When the bright healing light of his caring warms all of us taking us to a peak place that alters and changes our hearts in beautiful and permanent ways.

Q. What are the types of retreats and seminars that Contemplative Brothers offer?

A. Our retreats are centered on healing. We probe the deep contemplative depths of healing and the healing depths of contemplation and meditation. Much of what we do is to carry people on a journey or rather to let people know it's okay to go on the healing journey that the Lord is leading them on.

For instance, let's look at a parish mission. We come to the parish two or three

120.

days before Sunday masses begin, part of our way of preparation is to get to know the leaders in the parish, the pastor, the physical location, the geographic location, because each program we do is different. We try to make that program fit the people we are speaking to. Then on Sundays, we speak at all the Sunday masses, we give a talk usually after the Communion period. We give a talk on what will be coming up during the mission and we also usually lead people in a guided prayer experience. Every evening at the mission, we have a talk and guide people on prayer journey. This guiding of people on a prayer journey is a very ancient and biblical way of praying. We center our themes on drawing close to the Lord, themes of drawing close to each other and forgiving one another. We've seen some remarkable things happen.

People's Experiences on Retreat

Q. What are the types of experiences that occur on a mission?

A. I can tell you what happens. First of all, I want to say what happens to the people, what happens to their hearts, is not something that Robert or I or whoever else happens to be on the team does. We are just enablers, we're just witnesses. We are just witnesses to the one who really does bring healing, to the one who does bring closeness, to the one who brings reconciliation, the Lord himself. We are simply there to in some way stand by and observe that and to let people know it's okay to allow the Lord to work in their parish community and in their lives.

The first parish mission we gave was in Sauite-St. Marie, Canada in 1978. That ended up being an overwhelming experience for us. I am convinced of the power of deep healing prayer, deep meditative prayer, to open people up to the Lord's love. This was an inner city parish in Ontario made up, in part, of recent immigrants from Europe and ethnic neighborhoods. There were many Portuguese, many other ethnic groups, Polish, Italians, and in certain ways, a very traditional parish. The pastor there had done tremendous work and had excellent suggestions for us on how to do the mission. We spoke on the healing power of prayer and the beauty of our heritage as Christians at the Sunday masses and I looked out and found that just hearing about the way God can love us in deep prayer had touched people and there were tears everywhere. Something that really surprised me after the largest Mass, people began clapping very loudly as if to give a strong "Yes", a strong Amen. Then the rest of the week, except for the days the weather was bad, there was standing room only in that large parish.

What amazed me was the group that seemed the most enthusiastic were the younger teenagers. Before the parish mission began, we were asked to give a confirmation retreat for the young people from the Catholic schools. There were 60 eighth graders and we had never before given a retreat involving meditation to young people. I had given many youth retreats before but never on meditation. The pastor said just give a much shorter version of what you give to adults and I have a sense that remarkable things are going to happen.

We did that and after the first prayer experience, the young people wrote what they had experienced and hands were soon raised to share their experiences. I was shocked. The young people had had a profound experience of God's love and they were just vying with one another to stand up in front of their classmates and share what that experience was and throughout that mission, those young people showed up every night, sometimes dragging their parents along.

Also, the way the parish mission worked and the way our parish missions usually work, we try to keep the talk and the prayer experience short, sometimes the Eucharist is included, to an hour, because we know people have to get up early the next morning, we know people are tired from working all day and we believe in really keeping it brief. However, for those people that do want to stay longer and to share in a more personal way, we have a coffee time with coffee and doughnuts, people gather round, mingle, talk to one another, and then after that, we gather people into small groups and let them share personally about what is happening in their lives and what is happening on the mission. It is also a time for them to ask Robert and me questions that they want answers for.

I guess, too, one of the most beautiful experiences we had was seeing a very cold, rural parish become a very warm parish within a week. The people, all German descent, all caring people, very good people, but they didn't show their feelings very much. Church to them was a bit drab, in that it was more of a duty than a joy. We saw a remarkable change. By the end of the week, a powerful reconciliation had taken place in the parish. Some of the very conservative people and some of the very liberal people found how deeply they cared for each other and how deeply they could respect their differences and still love one another in God. By the end of the week, we found tears of prayer on people's eyes, a real warmth as people embraced each other.

Regional Engagements

Q. What is it like to do regional engagements?

A. I can tell you what those are like. The first really large regional engagement we gave was in 1978 in Southern California. I had been invited out by SCRC. SCRC is a ministry within the Archdiocese of Los Angeles but it also serves all of Southern California. They bring out speakers on spiritual topics, and on topics of renewal. I was asked to speak at a gathering of several hundred leaders in the Church in Southern California. I was asked to speak one morning to them and lead them through some prayer experiences.

The theme I talked about was how easy it is for people in ministry, especially lay people who are very involved within their churches, to lose energy, to burnout, and for that to hurt their families and their marriages. What was once a rich experience, without the restfulness of prayer can become a hesitant experience, a labored experience. Without allowing God to refresh us, without taking that time for him to renew us, without wasting time on the Lord, we'll get burned-out.

I talked about the powerful qualities of healing prayer, that just taking time to allow God to love us, take a sunbath in his love everyday, take that sunbath in His love with your family, with the people around you, take time to be lovingly present to your family and friends, take time to be lovingly present to God, waste time on family and one another, even if you have to cut back on what you are doing in ministry, the remaining part of your ministry will be so much more alive. Schedule time for this "re-creation" just as you schedule time for work.

Then we went to various regions the rest of the two weeks, various regions in Southern California, speaking at twilight retreats, that's an evening three-hour retreat, and speaking at several full days of renewal on the remaining two weekends. We spoke to thousands of people during that time.

I was touched by Father Ralph Tichenor, S.J., who has been such a spiritual father to us til his death. Father Tichenor, the head of SCRC, wrote that the renewal and the church in Southern California would never be the same after we left.

After we left on that first visit, they began to bring in other people, such as that wonderful teacher and healer, Father George Maloney, and others to help them grow in deep healing prayer and deep contemplative prayer. I was touched to the point of tears that Father Ralph had felt that we had so deeply touched the church. But I know it was not us that touched the church, just the simple power of gospel prayer, the simple power of healing prayer. We have made five ministry trips to Southern California since then.

You know, the deep meditation and the deep contemplation we are taking about are not things that are complex and hard, it is not a complicated way of praying, it is not the post-graduate work of Christian prayer. Rather, it is the simplest way of praying, the most direct way of praying, the most immediate contact with God. One of the things the great leaders and saints of the Church have been unanimous in is that the more we grow in prayer, the simpler our prayer becomes, until finally our prayer becomes a loving gaze of our heart upon God and his loving gaze upon us as we gaze into His very eyes. That is the place of healing and the place of prayer.

Individual Lives Changed

Q. You have discussed the changes that occur in group situations. Can you share some experiences concerning changes that have occurred in individual's lives?
A. Yes, Steve, I can. I guess the person that I think of the most when I talk about long term changes is Judy Esway. Judy attended one of the very first retreats we gave in Phoenix, Arizona. She had just moved there from Ohio. Her husband had been transferred. She had left her roots and hadn't really established roots yet where she was in Phoenix. She was a very faithful Catholic and had been involved in renewal movements. But yet at the same time, Judy missed a sense of rootedness in her faith, I believe. We saw Judy on that first retreat and we

123.

saw her face change from that first night. The first night, she had the harried look of a working mother who had several young children and has moved cross-country, bags under her eyes. The next day, a warm glow began to round out her face, her facial muscles were relaxed. We could see gentle tears of prayer and tears of healing going down her eyes. She was so excited about the retreat that the next week, when we were going to do a similar retreat in another part of Phoenix, she stayed home with the kids and insisted her husband go.

Judy later shared that one of the main healings she received was a greater ability to be affectionately close to people with warm embraces and touch. At least one of the things that happened in her is that since that time, she has felt free to fully embrace the people in her family, her friends, to feel their warmth.

Judy has become almost a part of us even though she is a full continent away from us. Since that time, we talk to her every two weeks by phone and we spent many times with her and her husband and they have visited us.

Judy followed up on her experience. She attended courses in theology and the theology of spiritual renewal at the Kino Institute, which is operated by the Carmelites in Phoenix. There are many other ministries beside the ministry that we have at Contemplative Brothers. People need to learn from those as much as they do from us. If we start them off, we are glad for them to be exposed to different approaches. Judy became very active in her diocese, active in adult ministry to the sick. Judy felt a real calling to write. Reading over her early attempts, I really worried about her being disappointed when she received rejection slips from publishers. But she combined her inner sense of firey love for God and people that had been taking place in her heart and the powerful feminine sensitivity to emotions that is part of her along with what she had learned from us and what she had learned from others and the theological footing she was gaining.

I was joyful when 23rd Publications told her that her first book would be coming out. It is called, **Prayers for Working Mothers**. It includes depth of insight and depth of emotion. She will be coming out with a much larger book in a year, that 23rd has asked her to do. I guess in Judy I find a sense of someone who has really progressed. Judy is someone who renews us and helps us by the power of her loving presence.

Q. That account you just shared about Judy Esway reminds me of the healing impact that Contemplative Brothers has had on my life from the moment I met you. I never knew what a personal God was until I learned to communicate in prayer with Him and learn what prayer was. I never had a real walk with God and my adjustments to life's hurts has taken a turn for the better because of the positive impact that your ministry has had on my life and many other people here in the local area have told me that just from attending your retreats and often times, just reading your material that they suddenly could bask in the warmth of God like they never have in their lives. The God of love and peace that had been preached and taught to them all these years was suddenly realized in their lives. For the first time in their lives, they had begun to feel healing occurring. I can just say from what I know personally and from what others have told me here, that your ministry is necessary and very much appreciated here in the local community.

A. Thank you, Steve, for what you are saying. That really touches me and it is so good to know that our work does touch people.

Retreat For U.S. Bishop's Liasons

Q. What is the most meaningful engagement that you have ever done?

A. Steve, that's very easy for me to answer. It's the one that scared me the most simply because of the people I'd be working with. In 1982, I received an invitation to take part in a theological symposium on renewal and contemplation. This symposium was part of the annual symposium offered by the U.S. Bishops' Liaisons. Each bishop in the Roman Catholic Church and appoints a person to be his vicar or his personal overseer, a liaison, of spiritual renewal within that diocese. They provide renewal movements such as marriage encounters and especially the charismatic renewal within their diocese. These liasons gather once a year in the spring of the year. They all come together and work on decisions that need to made, ideas, and then take time for prayer and deliberation about the direction of renewal in the United States.

Before their meeting in the spring, they have a much smaller meeting in the fall. That meeting is a theological symposium. They invite well-known theologians to present papers on a certain theme of renewal. They then present and discuss those at the symposium and those provide much of the theme and direction of the meeting of everyone later on. I was invited to be a presenter. When I knew who the other presenters were, I sometimes wondered if I was out of my league. There was Abbot Thomas Keating, the retired abbot of Spencer, Massachusetts who pioneered the centering prayer movement. He personally played so much of a role in the coming alive in an everyday way of contemplation. In addition to them, Father John Sheets, S.J., Father Paul Hinnebusch, O.P., and Sister Jean Hill, a Dominican nun who was one of the pioneers of healing ministry in the United States.

It was a wonderful time, that symposium. I was touched to the core that people of this stature gave me great affirmation in my work. That it was a time of real healing for me because to hear people with credentials such as theirs, warmly enthusiastic about what we were doing and hearing the wonderful exciting things they were doing. I must also add that Robert Herrmann attended the symposium. He attended as a participant, not as a presenter. Robert was asked to lead morning prayers for the group at the symposium one day. He lead them through a simple beautiful, guided imaginative journey into the woods and along a stream and then where people met Jesus and people who were important to them in their lives. After the symposium was over, the committee members who were in charge of the bishop's liaisons, took me and Robert aside, and said we want you to do something, and please try to find time on your calendar. They were touched by the meditation Robert led us in that they asked us to come to the full meeting of their national organization in the spring and lead all the liaisons in a day retreat and one day of prayer with many of these forms of prayer.

We did that and again received so much love and affirmation. We were so excited about all the things happening all over the church with healing and renewal that we saw in these leaders. Again I thought how beautiful and of the Lord's sense of humor. Robert Herrmann, whose furthest formal theological education is 8th grade Sunday School, was leading U.S. Bishops' representatives in prayer.

I just want to comment, it's off the question, but one of the things about Robert is Robert is a profoundly balanced person. He has helped me become balanced, something I needed in my life. Robert is an athlete, has placed in many local races, is a marathoner, has a wide variety of interests. He has a real gift of balance.

Programs for Young People

Q. I have heard that you do many retreats and seminars for young people? Isn't it odd that young people would be an audience for a seminar on prayer and contemplation?

A. We have given scores of retreats for young people and we find that young people anywhere from the 6th grade on up are the most open people for this type of prayer. Their imaginations are alive.

Yes, I would say that the most remarkable things that have happened that we have seen, the most remarkable retreats are with young people. In the fall of 1985, we gave a retreat for 300 young people in El Paso. It was part of the renewal convention for their diocese. We had them for three days. Most of them were Hispanic young people and maybe a fourth to a third of them had had powerful renewal experiences before but many of them were just dragged there. These were teenage young people, ninth grade age up through beginning college, the parents wanted to not have to take care of some children had even sneaked in a few older grammar school children here and there. As is the case with many Hispanic audiences, they have strong family ties and so we had many whole families, all the brothers and sisters and their cousins.

The bishop began the retreat for them, he gave a powerful and wonderful talk. We found that very quickly they moved into meditative prayer, that an ease took place in their muscles, their muscles became very deeply relaxed, a gentle hint of tears and moisture in their eyes, that the prayer experiences got to them in a very deep place. They very beautifully shared that with their peers and with one another.

Saturday evening was a profound time. We had been taking time for prayer and meditation all day and that night we just passed the microphone from one young person to another, and they shared some of their very deepest feelings, their deepest feelings of love of God, and love for their brothers and sisters. A common theme with the families that had several brothers and sisters was reconciliation. One family after another shared that they had really realized how much they meant to each other and that a brother or sister told that brother or sister that they loved them for the first time.

They shared very deep stories from their lives. One young man who I think was far more eloquent than any of us adult speakers, told of how close he was to his mother, how she loved him, what a rich experience he had of her and then of her death. He said, "You know, I have such a wonderful experience of love and mothering from my mother, but I haven't thought about that in years because, if I remembered the good things she gave me, if I remembered the influence she had on me, I opened myself to experience the pain of her loss. I'm now able to remember her goodness and celebrate it and I am able to feel the pain and know that that pain is shared. I am so glad that all of the other young people here have given me back the gift of my memories."

I also might add to, Steve, that with young epople, there are times when we give retreats for young people that it doesn't happen like that. There are times when I have been into CCD classes in high school and have had a regular Catholic high school class within 45 minutes. They were sharing deep things from their lives after a prayer experience. But with young people, peer pressure is an important factor, If I am tired or Robert is tired, or whoever is working in the retreat tired that particular day, it is easy to make this mistake. In the first few minutes, especially in the shorter periods that we have, where we speak at schools, if we aren't able to gently turn the peer pressure toward the side of openness, the retreat can be a good experience still, but less dramatic and open.

Weekend Retreats For Adults

Q. I have also heard that you do weekend retreats. What exactly happens on these?

A. We really love to do weekend retreats, Steve, and we especially like to do them in retreat houses where people can actually spend the night. We just had a very powerful retreat in Detroit, Michigan that was very meaningful to us at Duns Scotus. We also sometimes, when it is not possible for everyone to have a location such as a retreat house where they can spend the night, people come to the retreat during the day and in the evening and go home. But we do find that the warm friendships that are formed on that retreat plus the intensity of experience and the healing quality can be much deeper because it is concentrated.

The Place of Balance

Q. How do you manage all your work and activities?

A. Balance is important for us. I was too one-sided when I first began this ministry. I wanted to pray all the time and study all the time. Now I find that taking a time everyday for cycling or running is just as important as my prayer time. Balance is so important. Taking time to be with friends, taking time for vacation, taking time for physical exercise and the right diet, are just as important as my reading of scripture. I have always had a problem in my adult life of being overweight and, thanks to Robert Herrmann and his athletic knowledge and ability, I am in very good physical shape.

Even though I am still too overweight, I can cycle 20 miles and barely get winded. I feel vibrant and alive. I know that is as much a result of physical exercise as anything else.

Another thing I think is very important is simple, boring tasks that seem so hard on us; cleaning the house, cleaning your room, writing letters, answering phone calls, that in a very real way, those ground us to this world. So often the people of prayer in the church were profoundly practical people. They knew how to plan things. They were very pragmatic. They knew how to use a broom. I think that is an important aspect of our lives, and one that I am slowly learning.

Indian Heritage

And I must say one other thing, too, about balance in our lives. Both Robert and I are part native American. We are both formally enrolled in one of the bands of the Cherokee tribe. My Indian heritage means so much to me and my very earliest and deepest memories are of my Cherokee grandfather and the stories of our people that he passed on to me. He could not read or write, but yet he is the wisest man I have ever known. He was a Christian but he kept many Indian ways that are so comparable to the New Testament. People ask me what is Indian spirituality? and I say look at the Sermon on the Mount and look at the life of St. Francis and then you will know what native American spirituality is all about. He lived that-a closeness to nature, a closeness to people, a simplicity of life. He formed me in the wisdom of my people very early. About every three weeks, I gather on a farm together with other Christians who are of native American descent as well as others interested in our ways, our culture, and our prayer. We spend a weekend together and we pray together and we go to the sweat lodge and doing our healing prayer in that lodge with hot stones, wearing bathing suits and sweating. It is very different from our weekly praying in churches in modern buildings. Here we are close to nature, we are close to our earthiness, we are vulnerable. We pray to the Creator, the God and Father of our Lord, Jesus Christ to come into our hearts and I am so grateful for this loving group of people that love us into wholeness so many times when we are tired. They mean so much to us. One friend was describing for another what it was like to pray with our native American friends and said, "You know what the great healing of retreat is like, how the warmth of that retreat is so beautiful, at the end of the retreat? Well, stepping on the porch of Jerome and Clare Ennis, the Creek and Cherokee couple that own the farm, for the first time you feel the same warm safe feelings that you feel at the end of a weekend retreat, there is so much love. So many times, the love of this wonderful and human couple has been a refuge we enter, to be refreshed when the worries of the world weigh us down.

Afterword

For most people today the idea of contemplation conjures up extremely negative or unpleasant ideas, probably because it sounds so much like a withdrawal from life, and these days advertisements tell us to grab all the gusto we can. Or perhaps it sounds mysterious, monkish or out of the Middle Ages, and no longer of any relevance for a technological society. Nothing could be farther from the truth. I fact, the hurry and mechanization of our day have cut us off from our own depths and hence the source of our strength. But we must find ourselves as God's creations, loved by him and redeemed by Christ. In this true life is found. **Prayer That Heals Our Emotions** by Eddie Ensley is a book designed to help you find that life. It is a simple (but not simplistic), moving, helpful volume that offers concrete suggestions as to how contemplation can deepen your life, even though you must go on living in the hectic "real world" of today.

By Dr. Walter Elwell,
(dean of the graduate school of Religion,
Wheaton College, editor of the
Evangelical Theological Dictionary)

Bearing Witness

In the Fall of 1984 Contemplative Brothers conducted a weekend retreat for the renewal movement in the diocese of Cleveland. Those who were there wrote summaries of their experiences:

"This weekend has been the most cleansing, pleasing and stress free time I can ever recall. At least its been many years. I have been re-aquainted with many loves I had long forgotten ... I've truly touched the hem of his garment and have been baptized in the river Jordan."

Patricia P

"I have been on several inner healing retreats over the last 3 years. However, none has been as meaningful as this retreat was. Your approach and methods are slower paced, and you allow the Lord to reveal a memory that needs healing, rather than making suggestions or taking a life's's walk. ... Also, the end of the retreat with the session on healing the world and sharing one another's burdens, in an area of healing that is too often overlooked."

Lois W

"The weekend was excellent, extraordinary group experience. I got in touch with my true self and had the experience of seeing God cleanse me of many things that blocked my relationship with Him. Neveer have I seen so many people truly and deeply touched by almighty God. I believe everyone is changed and made new in an extraordinary way that is impossible to put into words. We would need to write volumes of shared experiences to do justice to Almight God's Work. Grace, and New Life!"

Dolores H.

"Your healing week-end here in Cleveland confirms my prayers and beliefs that healing can and must occur in large groups coming together in prayer. In my own experience and in working with so many people suffering physical illness and emotional distress I am convinced of the great need for your work.

Eventually, the answers to all our pain and all our problems are spiritual answers. This week-end is the best approach I have yet experienced to introduce and minister to large groups the healing power and love of the Lord."

Tom W.

How To Bring Healing Retreats To Your Area

Starting in 1987 we have some dates available to bring retreats, missions and programs on prayer and healing to different areas of the country. We are especially open to renewal conferences. We are not able to take every invitation, but we will prayerfully consider every invitation and will get in touch with you soon after we hear from you. Write us or call us with your proposed dates and be sure to tell us about yourself and your area.

Phone (404) 689-1892
CONTEMPLATIVE BROTHERS
Box 8065
Columbus, GA 31908

Cassettes For the Inner Journey

The following meditation, 5 series cassets have similar material to the guided meditations in this book.

Beautiful music, sounds from nature provide background for a powerful journey of healing. You may order them for a 10-day, risk-free examination period.

1. **Prayer That Heals Our Emotions.** These 3 cassettes lead you into deep prayerful relaxation and help you experience a new level of inner harmony. Price $23.95.

2. **Prayer That Heals Relationships.** Based on meditations similar to the material in this book on relationships. The meditations help you discover how to express love more freely and how to let love in. Price $23.95.

3. **Experiencing God's Nearness In The Gospels.** This series of 3 tapes leads you into guided meditations based on Gospel scenes. The tapes massage your busy body and tense mind with comforting scenes from Scripture. Price $23.95.

4. **Making Peace With The Past.** Helps you open your heart to the experience of inner healing. Helps you open to God's healing of past hurts. Price $23.95.

5. **Healing Ourselves; Healing Our World.** Based on meditations in the section of this book with the same name. Price 23.95.

To order: Send us your name, phone number and address along with the titles you are ordering. Listen to the tapes for up to 10 days. If after 10 days, they have helped you; send payment along with the invoice; if not, send the tapes back within the 10-day period and pay nothing and owe nothing.

Contemplative Brothers
Dept. F-1, Box 8065
Columbus, GA 31908

About The Author

Eddie Ensley received his B.A. in Philosophy and Biblical studies from Belhaven College.

He completed three years post-graduate work in theology plus an additional year in studying counseling and history. The director of Contemplative Brothers he has conducted numerous retreats and programs throughout the United States, Canada, the Carribean and Mexico. He was a presenter at the U.S. Bishops' Liasons Theological Symposium.

He is the author of **Sounds of Wonder** *(Paulist Press),* **Healing Pathways** *(Contemplative Books) and* **The Charismatic Renewal and Contemplation** *(co-author along with Paul Hinnebusch O.P., Abbot Thomas Keating and others, Paulist Press.)*

Of Cherokee descent, an enrolled member of the Echota Cherokee tribe. Active in promoting native American culture, he is a member of the Cherokee National Historical Society.

Over a 100,000 cassettes of Eddie's guided prayer experiences have been sold.